Cuba at Sea

Figure 1: Ron Ridenour destroyed his US passport January 17, 1991, in front of the United States Interests Section in Havana, in protest of its attack upon Iraq.

Cuba at Sea

Ron Ridenour

Socialist Resistance

Also by Ron Ridenour

"Cuba: Beyond the Crossroads"

"Cuba: A "Yankee" Reports"

"Backfire: The CIA's Biggest Burn"

"Cuba at the Crossroads"

"Yankee Sandinistas"

"Revolutionære Visioner"; Co-author

"Eyes See What Eyes Want to See: Western Media and the Peace Movement"; Co-author

"Mood Pictures from a Central American Peace March, Glass House Tapes"; Co-author

The author's website is at www.ronridenour.com. He can be contacted by email at ronr@mail.dk.

Socialist Resistance would be glad to have readers' opinions of this book, its design and translations, and any suggestions you may have for future publications or wider distribution.

Socialist Resistance books are available at special quantity discounts to educational and non-profit organizations, and to bookstores.

To contact us, please write to Socialist Resistance, PO Box 1109, London, N4 2UU, Britain, email contact@socialistresistance.net or visit socialistresistance.net.

Published by Socialist Resistance, May 1st, 2008.
Printed in Britain by Lightning Source.
ISBN   978-0-902869-91-2

CONTENTS

Also by Ron Ridenour 4
CONTENTS 5
Photographs 5
ACKNOWLEDGMENTS 6
INTRODUCTION: COMING HOME 7
CHAPTER ONE: SEAWEED 16
CHAPTER TWO: PORT SANTIAGO DE CUBA 40
CHAPTER THREE: PORT CIENFUEGOS 45
CHAPTER FOUR: SEAWEED RETIRES 55
CHAPTER FIVE: SHARK 59
CHAPTER SIX: GIORITA: Sailing to Europe 71
CHAPTER SEVEN: ROSE ISLANDS Return to Cuba 100
CUBA: TENACIOUS ROYAL PALM 108

Photographs

Figure 1: Ron Ridenour destroyed his US passport January 17, 1991, before the United States Interests Section in Havana, in protest of its attack upon Iraq 2
Figure 2: To be Internationalist is to settle our own debt with humanity 7
Figure 3: Ron Ridenour is greeted by one of the Cuban double agents 10
Figure 4: Ron burning his US passport January 17, 1991, in front of the United States Interests Section in Havana, in protest of its attack upon Iraq 15
Figure 5: Ron Ridenour at the helm of 'Seaweed' 16
Figure 6: Ron working on "Seaweed", Cuba, 1991 40
Figure 7: Sailing past Havana harbor and fort 57
Figure 8: Captain Antonio Garcia Urquiolla. He had been a double agent within the CIA for Cuba's defense, and figures in Ridenour's book, "Backfire: The CIA's Biggest Burn" 59
Figure 9: Throwing line to anchor, "Shark", 1990 63
Figure 10: A seaman painting "Shark", 1990 67
Figure 11: Coast guard picking up rafters headed towards Miami, 1990 68
Figure 12: Giorita on way to Holland from Cuba, 1992 71
Figure 13: Giorita Captain Carlos García spying Gibraltar, 1992 92
Figure 14: Minister of Communications, Manuel Castillo Rebasa, explains to journalists in Havana that the U.S. television signal, TV Martí, as they call it and which Cubans call aggression TV (telegresión), is about to be launch that morning, March 25, 1990 96
Figure 15: Ron returns to Cuba on "Rose Islands", May 1993 99
Figure 16: "Rose Islands", Holland-Cuba, May 1993 101
Figure 17: Diploma for the volunteer deckhand 107

ACKNOWLEDGMENTS

The events and facts described herein are real. I have changed some names and mixed some conversations into one dialogue, but without changing the meaning. On some occasions, terms for persons appear to be racial, calling someone by his skin color: black, mulato, white, Chinaman. In Cuban Spanish, these terms are not derogatory, rather expressions of identification and even often of affection. Sometimes, however, prejudice can be associated with such terminology, depending on attitude and tone. The reader should not deduce that I am always in agreement with points of view expressed. I have intended to paint pictures of the overall society.

I owe gratitude to many Cubans, and to the Argentine Che Guevara, who were my midwives to internationalist philosophy and into action against injustice and imperialism. I also thank the administrators of Caribe, Mambisa, the Ministry of Transport, and la Dirección de Orientación de la Revolución (DOR)—organ of the Communist Party Central Committee—for conceding permission for me to navigate with the nation's ships. In the years following my collaboration with these entities many of them have changed structures and names. Most international shipping is now, in 2008, conducted as joint ventures with foreign capital. Cuban ships are either owned or co-owned with foreign firms, and some fly foreign flags.

I thank Socialist Resistance for its interest in publishing the manuscript, and especially Duncan Chapel for his design and coordination. The manuscript originally was planned for publication in Cuba but with the economic downturn and the tightening of publications under the "special period", it was not possible to be published. Now, with some updating, it finally sees the light of day.

I especially appreciate the officers and crew of the ships: Seaweed, Shark, Gold Star, Giorita and Rose Islands. These merchant marines accepted me as a member of their families. They gave me access and space to engage myself as I wished, in order to fulfill my curiosity and assist in my writings. In large part, the book is inspired by the valiant crew of the small cargo ship Hermann, which withstood violent attacks by a US coast guard gunboat:

Captain Diego Sanchez Serrano
Héctor Maura Díaz
Santiago Rodríguez Maya
Héctor González Pagés
Jesús Dole Calzadilla
Jacinto Farnot Camilo
Lino de la Luz Reyes Rosell
Mario Andrés Hidalgo Olívera
Francisco Montalvo Peñalver
Osvaldo Santíago Vega
Annel Bertot Gutiérrez

INTRODUCTION: COMING HOME

Figure 2: To be Internationalist is to settle our own debt with humanity

This billboard is the first one I remember seeing after landing in Havana. No better slogan could express my own feelings and morality than this statement of conscience. I was Home!

It started with a phone call. The year was 1987 and I lived in Copenhagen.

"Hello. This is the Cuban embassy. May I help you?" the woman answered in broken English.

"Yes. I am Ron Ridenour. I wish to speak with the consul about a trip to Cuba," I replied in Spanish.

"Yes. I am the ambassador. Marta Jímenez Martínez at your service."

I hesitated. I had expected to be answered by a clerk, a secretary, not the number one representative of their country. That was not what we experience at any other embassy. I explained my interest in contacting them and was cordially invited to stop by.

Some background to the phone call is necessary. I had made an agreement with an El Salvadorian guerrilla commandant to travel with liberation fighters. I would observe how the people lived and fought, in order to write a book. I would present their cause to other parts of the world. In order to complete this mission, I needed to come inside clandestinely. The government would not grant me—a revolutionary journalist noted in the empire's intelligence archives—permission to enter the country and write about the oppression and the dirty war they conducted against the people. I would fly to Cuba first, then to Mexico and from there inside El Salvador.

I had never been to Cuba. But it was Cuba's revolution that woke me up. The first time I demonstrated was in protest over the US attack on Cuba at the Bay of Pigs. I picketed the Federal Building in Los Angeles, on April 19, 1961. I joined the Fair Play for Cuba Committee. I wrote articles in a college underground newspaper I helped start, "The Raven", about the new government's efforts to abolish racism and end poverty. It only seemed natural that the self-declared greatest democracy would aid these humanitarian practices. Instead, the US government attacked these very humanitarian policies and even invaded the country on April 17, 1961.

The FBI and CIA began following me and labeled my actions subversive. Cubans struggle to feed everyone, provide free education and health care for all, fight for national independence, and the US's reactions against this goodness led me to understand what my country was actually about. I was angry and still am.

I came to the Cuban embassy with my CV and a copy of my recently published book on Nicaragua, "Yankee Sandinista". I hoped that the book would help identify me and my politics for the Cubans. It did.

The embassy employed five people. Besides the ambassador, there was her guajiro (1) husband, Luís García., their public relations representative, Rogerio "Jimmy" Santana, his wife Carmen, and a chauffeur and handyman whose name I can't remember. They all wanted a copy of my book and bought extras. They weren't just individual employees. They were family in blood and in spirit. They accepted me as one of them. They assisted me with enthusiasm; helped my travel plans and added to them.

The Cuban government had just revealed the identity of 27 double agents, workers who had been recruited by the CIA to spy upon their country and sabotage it. They had accepted the offers and immediately informed their government. The 26 Cubans and one Italian then became double agents for their people. This became the subject of a book I would write, "Backfire: The CIA's Biggest Burn".

Jimmy sent copies of "Yankee Sandinistas" to the ministries of culture and foreign relations, and told me to look up the foreign book publisher, Editorial José Martí. Maybe they would want to publish the book and maybe I might write something about the double agents. Jimmy also introduced me to Barbara Dane, an American folk singer whom I knew indirectly from the Vietnam War days in the USA. I first met her when she came to Denmark to perform. Barbara was also the mother of Pablo Menendéz, who had become a Cuban citizen. He was married to Adría Santana, a nationally known actress and Jimmy's sister. My wife, Grethe Porsgaard, and I could live with them when we came to Cuba.

One September morning, in 1987, Grethe and I landed in Havana's José Martí airport. We took a taxi to Adría and Pablo's house in La Playa area of Havana. Their plant-covered duplex, slightly shaded from the simmering sun by palm fronds, overlooked the warm Caribbean splashing on a sandy beach. We spent an exciting month with them before Grethe returned to Denmark to her work and I went to El Salvador. In that first month, I heard Fidel Castro "perform" a speech in the parliament. It was my first of many live speeches by this master orator. I was mesmerized by his folksy style and his breadth of knowledge about the world. He spoke for four hours without notes, without water. I could have listened longer.

I was warmly welcomed at Editorial José Martí by the director, Félix Sautié Mederos, and chief editor, Iván Pérez Carrión. They took a copy of "Yankee Sandinistas" to read. They asked me if I would like to interview some of the double agents. They wanted to publish a book about them and what the CIA had set them to do against their country. I could write a chapter. When I interviewed the first two, a married couple who had worked for Cuban airlines, I was so impressed with their courage, their dignity and loyalty that I fell in love with these people. (2)

The first remarkable trait I noticed about Cubans is their erect stature and shinning eyes, which emit a sense of self-worth and equality among all humans. People old enough to have lived under the Batista dictatorship and neo-colonialism had long surpassed the state of inequality among humans of different economic and racial status. The young had never been taught that they must bow down before "superiors." Old and young alike of all colors look everyone in the eyes. And they all take pride in their personal appearance, in corporal cleanliness and clean clothing.

In my next visit to the publishing house, I was offered a contract to publish "Yankee Sandinistas" in Spanish. That was good news but that wasn't all. I reported what I was learning from the double agents and they asked me to write a book about them. I was elated.

Soon, it was time for me to take a flight to Mexico. Depending on what occurred in El Salvador, I might have time to gather more interviews and other material for the double agents book upon returning to Cuba, en route to Denmark. I waited about two months in Mexico before receiving word to enter El Salvador. During this time, I wrote for the English language weekly magazine, Mexican Review, published by the prestigious left-wing daily newspaper, "La Jornada."

My first contact with an El Salvadorian guerrilla took place smack-dab in front of a major military base in the capital city. She stepped off a public bus wearing smart clothing. Young, attractive, she appeared to be a middle class woman. We strolled across the street from the heavily guarded, walled-in base.

"I almost got robbed on that bus," she told me with a laugh. "Imagine me, an experienced guerrilla getting my purse stolen by a bus thief! I discovered his hand just in time. Come, we'll get some coffee and talk."

The nature of the warring conflict had changed since a year ago when our plans were hatched. The Yankees had stepped up their aggressive support of the puppet regime. There were more pressing needs than the book project, which would take one or two years before publication. They asked me to help with cultural solidarity work in Denmark. I was not enthused but agreed to do one specific project upon my return. Now that I would not be traveling with the guerrillas, the next several months were open. I decided to return to Cuba and complete interviewing and gathering material for the double agent book.

I returned to Pablo and Adría's home. I set up more interviews and the Ministry of Interior gave me some access to information on CIA subversion from their Office of Interest in Havana. Some of the coded information from both sides was made available. Shortly before I was to return to Denmark, where I would write the book, the publishing house and I signed the book contract, and they extended yet another exciting offer: a job as a "foreign technician," performing editing and writing functions. The terms of both contracts were generous. I would be paid 12 pesos per page delivered. This resulted in an average wage for about 18 months. I would be paid 310 pesos monthly as a contracted worker, half again the average wage and equivalent to what professional Cuban editors make. I would also be provided with an apartment where Cubans live, a ration food and clothing card, which all Cubans have, and other benefits of socialism, such as free medical care. Grethe could live with me and our flight to and fro would be paid for. It was an offer of a lifetime.

Just before leaving for Denmark, I heard Pablo's tale of coming to Cuba and staying. His story coincided with some of my own feelings and experiences. One difference, however, was that his mother was the first American artist to break the blockade by conducting a musical tour of Cuba.

Pablo explained internationalism for me in a way that made the billboard real.

"I've sacrificed the need that most people have of identifying with one country, and gained the sense of being part of two countries, in fact, the whole world. The minute I'm in any country, I identify with the problems, hopes and visions of those people. I don't really feel marginal but internationalist. Cuba has ten million people cultivating internationalist feelings. So, everybody here understands me when I play in a concert."

Back in Denmark, I began writing the manuscript. Grethe decided not to live with me in Cuba but would come for extended visits. When I finished the first draft, Grethe and I traveled to New York City. The US media had published precious little about the largest infiltration and undermining of CIA "dirty tricks" in its 40 year history. A new producer at CBS 60-Minutes, Karen Taylor, was interested in the story and she contacted me. Taylor finally told me that top management, "won't go with the story unless we get independent verification." Such "verification" must come from some United States government or congressional source. The CIA was mute, as they always are, and no other government or congressional branch saw any gain in participating. So, "the story is dead", Taylor concluded.

Figure 3: Ron Ridenour is greeted by one of the Cuban double agents

Grethe returned to Denmark and I went on to Cuba. Two publishing house employees picked me up at the airport. They were most surprised to see that I had my bicycle with me. This was before the oil shortage and before Cuba became known for having so many cyclists. But I had learned on my first trip that relying on public transportation would slow me down much more than my energy flow could tolerate. While the publishing house completed its end of the contract by sending me plane tickets on time, it had not arranged for a place for me to live. I later learned that this was normal procedure because the custom is not to rely on anyone until he or she shows up. I certainly couldn't complain since they arranged for me to stay at a modest hotel, the Lincoln, used mainly by Cubans on vacation. I ended by staying there three months, including one month with Grethe when she came to visit. Accommodations were fine. The only drawback was the long wait for each meal. My room and board were paid for so I almost always ate at the hotel. I finished doing research and a rewrite of the book at the hotel.

I was moved into Cuba's tallest building, Focsa. This 30-story apartment building is a triangle which meets on a corner in downtown Havana. It was built in the 1950s to be a fashionable place for the more well-to-do, but after the revolution poorer Cubans filled the building. By the 1990s, the occupants were Cubans and foreign technicians like me. Most of the latter were from the Comecon countries.

My editor and the director approved "Backfire: The CIA's Biggest Burn", and started the publishing process, said to take a year. I met some Cuban authors who told me not to hold my breath. Most books took from three to five years to come out. While I waited, I volunteered to work in a construction brigade building an apartment building. There would be 12 apartments; half would go to employees of the publishing house, which took responsibility to do some of the work, and the other half would go to the housing ministry, which would assign the other apartments to people on a waiting list. I also volunteered in agriculture, cultivating vegetables, harvesting bananas and chopping sugar cane.

Chopping sugar cane with a machete is one of the toughest jobs in the world: sweltering hot, back-breaking, and shin-cutting. But I loved doing it. Of course, I only worked for a week or two at a time. That makes a big difference in one's "loving" attitude.

Sautié suggested that I experience Cuba as much as I wished and then write a book about Cuba seen from my eyes. This was a wonderful idea, one that gave me almost complete freedom. I came up with the idea of seeing Cuba from both land and sea. I would travel to all the provinces on bicycle, train, bus, car and airplane. I would interview people, and do some volunteer work to get to know people and their living conditions better. I would sail around the island, working and seeing Cuba from seamen's eyes. I definitely wanted to sail with Captain Antonio García Urquiola, who had been a double agent and whom I had interviewed for "Backfire". Sautié approved the idea and wrote letters to the Caribe shipping company. But there were many institutions involved before final approval could be obtained. I write about paperwork bureaucracy in chapter six; and we meet Captain Urquiola and his ship, Shark, in chapter five.

I lived like Cubans did. My ration card could buy the same limited goods; the same scare and cheaply made clothes; the same cigars, rum and beer "when available". I had to queue up in the same long slow lines. My work conditions, wages and benefits were the same. Different from the norm, however, was that with this assignment I had almost total say over what I did. I also did some free lance journalism. I could also save a bit from my wage. As a foreign technician, I did have a couple benefits most Cubans did not. There were a couple places open only to us where we could buy a decent meal and drink decent rum *"cuando hay"* (3). I could receive and use dollars, which I did when doing free lance reportage. (This possibility was granted all Cubans in July 1993.) I did short broadcasts for the only non-commercial and somewhat progressive radio network in the United States, Pacifica Radio. I also wrote news analysis and features for an English monthly, "South", and a piece here or there. (After my time sailing was over, I would become the English daily "Morning Star" correspondent alongside with my editorial-translating job at Cuba's foreign news service, Prensa Latina.) The few dollars I obtained from these sources went to buy one or two good bottles of rum a month. I saved the rest for future travel, for which dollars are essential.

When the biggest scandal in Cuba's revolutionary history occurred, I called in stories to Pacifica, stories such as this one, broadcast June 23, 1989:

"The Cuban government announced yesterday preliminary results of its investigation involving three officials in the army and 11 in the Ministry of Interior. Following tips from Cuban informants and friends of Cuba, the government discovered that army General Arnaldo Ochoa, Ministry of Interior General Patricio de la Guardia and his brother, Colonel Antonio de la Guardia Font, and a score other officers, had been misappropriating state funds and operating a drug racket for the past three years. The illegal activities netted the Cubans only $3.5 million.

"Fifteen successful operations were completed involving six tons of cocaine and a lesser amount of marijuana. The drugs came from the notorious Pablo Escobar Colombia cartel, and were flown to the Cuban resort in Varadero using a commercial trade cover under Antonio la Guardia control. The drugs were then transported to Miami in United States speed boats, the kind the CIA uses in attacking Cuba...

"The U.S. government began claiming in 1980 that Cuba's government and President Fidel Castro are drug traffickers. The Cuban government responded yesterday that this is the first case of drug trafficking. It said the criminals were captivated by the dazzling consumer society and its trinkets, and there was no political motivation.

"The drug scandal is extremely damaging to Cuba. General Ochoa is only one of two heroes holding the Medal of Honor. He was a key general in Cuban international operations in Nicaragua, Angola and Ethiopia..."

It was Fidel who initiated the investigation into possible drug smuggling. This was the first time such serious criminal activity had occurred since the revolutionary victory, and was especially painful and embarrassing to the president and the vast majority of Cubans. It is illegal to grow, sell and use any intoxicating drug, other than for medical reasons. And there was almost no drug taking in Cuba, not even marijuana. By reading foreign wire services—a part of his daily routine—,Fidel discovered that a former Cuban citizen, Reinaldo Ruíz, claimed in a Miami court case that he worked with Cuban military officials and drug magnate Pablo Escobar. He alleged that they carried "cocaine in a light plane," with stopovers in Cuba. Within a few months, the government put its case together and arrested the 14. They all confessed. A trial was conducted anyway, which is Cuba law. They were found guilty and the leading four officers and organizers were executed within the month. The others were given long prison sentences. The death penalty is rarely used but for this high crime it was employed after the supreme court rendered its affirmation, which is required in death penalty cases, and after the entire Council of State passed its judgment, also required for taking lives. This decision was especially painful to Fidel since he felt so close to Ochoa.

I was also saddened by this turn of events and decided to take a bike trip to Santa Clara, home of Che Guevara's museum. The 600-kilometer round trip also gave me good opportunity to speak with people about the drug case and how the government handled it. People were shocked and baffled about how such a gruesome crime could be pulled off, given that the executive government and MININT (Ministry of Interior) exercised as much control as they do, and given how much the leadership is opposed to drugs.

It was revealed during the trial that the government had attempted to dodge the strict US trading blockade by establishing, in 1982, a clandestine department, MC, within MININT, in order to quietly implement commercial operations with US citizens. Cuba sought to acquire medical and laboratory equipment, medicines and sanitary material, computers and other technological equipment and parts. MC had a blank check. It was the only entity that could get goods transported into the country without the obligatory customs checks. And that gave these men the opportunity to cheat. As the state prosecutor said in the trial summary, its ring leader had "the country's airways at his disposal; he had the authority to violate all the migration provisions; he allowed notorious criminals to enter the country and hid them here; and he was capable of preventing the authorities from taking action."

Why were these men given so much authority? Even worse, "How is it possible that our society can produce people who think and act as if they are above it?" asked a young member of the Council of State.

A colleague of mine had been a translator for Ochoa in Ethiopia. He explained that some high officials simply have carte blanche power in some circumstances. General Ochoa, he said, was already corrupt in 1977. He shopped in Europe for the best made Mercedes Benz, laced in gold. When his new car was being transported by ship to Ethiopia, Ochoa demanded that that ship be docked ahead of several others ships set to unload war materials the country needed in the war with Somalia. Ochoa and my colleague watched his orders be carried out. When the car was lifted down, they got in and drove off. Ochoa also made gifts of cases of Chivas Regal whiskey and expensive pens and watches.

It was impossible, however, to go over Ochoa's head and complain to higher authorities. There were none in Ethiopia. My friend questioned how Ochoa could have risen so high and kept on rising despite his "character deficiencies" of which the top leaders were then speaking.

The Cuban revolution was constantly instructing people to be righteous with one another, to stamp out individual greed. But there were holes in the Cuban system, and one of them was this broad flexibility in trying to overcome the strangling blockade.

Another compromising element from the capitalist world, which penetrates Cuba, is international advertising for the consumer society, which strongly competes with collectivist sharing values. As some Cuban Marxist philosophers I got to know said: You can't build true socialism on an island in a world dominated by its opposite.

One of the new voices of this contradiction, Mikhail Gorbachov, came to Cuba that year on a state visit. He was not loved by Cuba's politically conscious people, including the leadership. Many thought the CIA had gotten to him. He was leading the Soviet Union into the world of capitalism, and it wouldn't be long before the socialistic system fell apart.

I finally was granted permission to sail in the summer of 1990. I was told that this was a first for the Cuban government, allowing a foreigner not in Comecon to sail on one of their ships. Only Comecon ship technicians had been allowed. This was to be a unique experience and honor.

I had not sailed much when "Backfire" came out but I had earned the right to wear the seamen's tan uniform. We held the launching at the Ministry of Interior's museum, the most appropriate place given the subject matter and the collection of material they had on CIA subversion against their land. I stood before a large gathering of double agent "subjects", publishing employees, media folk and others in my new seamen's uniform. This was my proudest moment. I felt I had done something significant to expose the covert warrior-murderers from the country I had been born in. My editor spoke about the book's contents. I said that I felt part of their revolution and yearned to do more for it. Then one of the doubles, Jesús Francisco Díaz ("Dionisio"), spoke. I was honored by his appreciative words, by his and the others' presence.

A month later, I burned by passport in front of the United States Interests Section in Havana, in protest against the US invasion of Iraq. It was a lone action but the media carried it, both nationally and internationally. I acted out of sheer anger and frustration at having protested one US war after another. I later heard from people who had seen CNN's report in Europe, Australia, China and other places. One of my sons sat in his university dorm and watched with aggravation as his father burned the eagle-emblazoned symbol of imperial war. I could no longer stand to be a citizen of the policeman of the world.

I tried other possibilities to obtain a passport elsewhere. Cuba was not tactically wise since there would be countries, especially the US, where I could not travel. I tried Denmark without success since I had to be living there. Nor would the UN grant me a refugee travel pass. A year later, I would apply and receive a temporary US passport, which I had to renew each year, "if you don't burn it," wrote the State Department.

I did not want to return to the United States for many reasons, at least one was the people. I had come to appreciate Cuban people much more than any other population I knew.

Cubans are warm and amiable, usually helpful in times of need, and always ready to party. I relate an anecdote, which explains the significance of this national pastime and Cuba's folksy Marxism.

An acquaintance, Orlando Licea Díaz, came by my apartment to discuss the state of human affairs around the time I burned my passport. He was an erudite Marxist psychologist, who treated asthma patients. He invited me to Havana University's psychology college where he was to lecture psychologists and students on the psychological implications of José Martí thoughts. (He said that he had read the complete works of Martí and Marx several times.) The occasion was the national celebration of Martí's birthday. As we entered the college, an organizer of the event informed Licea that the speeches had just been canceled. "We're partying instead," she said, her brilliant eyes smiling rum.

"Great. Let's go get a drink and dance, Ron," he said gleefully and without hesitation.

When he saw my fallen face, he said, "Don't be sad. There'll be another occasion for this lecture. I'd rather drink and dance than give a speech any day."

Orlando was handed a large glass of beer, a rarity, and I another. Rum was abundant so beer was first choice. Many people greeted Orlando while he surveyed the hall for a pretty woman to dance with. He left me standing in silence while he danced. When he returned, he said, "I've found a new lover for tonight. Find a woman and let's dance."

"You can't let them just drop the importance of a lecture on Martí's day. You spent hours preparing. Canceling serious subject matters for partying is irresponsible," I protested

"You'll never understand what it is to be a Cuban until you learn that enjoying life—a woman's supple arms about you on a dance floor and a glass of rum—is far more satisfying than academic regimentation or `fulfilling one's duty'. Those are Germanic-European traits which only constrict people, making them uptight and, eventually, renegades to Marxism. Our marxism (with a small m) is tropical, taking in the natural course of life. This very fact—that it is more real, meaning more human—is why it is more solid. There will always be other times for lectures. Now we party!"

I had begun sailing by that time, and was ashore for a few days. I began to learn from seamen that Licea's analysis and appreciation of the Cuban culture is one very important reason why its socialism has not fallen apart as it has in the rest of the world.

Notes:

1. Small farmer.

2. "Never before have so many moles so completely fooled an intelligence agency for so long, obtaining volumes of data, spy equipment, and audio-visual proof of espionage and covert operations against their nation. The average agent (of these 27 who came out of the cold) worked clandestinely inside the CIA for 15 years, the longest for 21 years. Never did the stealthy CIA detect one of these double agents. The CIA suffered such loss of face and real material damage that it was rendered useless in Cuba, at least for a time." From Backfire, page 18.

3. When there is some.

Figure 4: Ron burning his US passport January 17, 1991, in front of the United States Interests Section in Havana, in protest of its attack upon Iraq

CHAPTER ONE: SEAWEED

Figure 5: Ron Ridenour at the helm of 'Seaweed'

Incipient rays of sun rose over our port bow illuminating the aqua Atlantic.

"015 starboard", commands the first mate, Sigi.

"Aye, 015 degrees starboard," I reply from the helm as I steer the Seaweed to a new course.

"Fifteen degrees starboard. Course now 1 5 0 degrees," I declare when the compass registers the new bearing. This medium size Soviet-built tanker is sailing at 12 knots.

"Steady as she goes," Sigi responds.

At the burst of brightness, the stocky, balding and graying seaman and I stand side by side in the pilot house. Six decks above water line, we watch sardine-size flying fish skipping just above the sea. Following their trajectory, we see the silhouette of a chair-shaped, low mountain.

"There it is, la Silla de Gibara, exclaims a smiling Sigi, "the first Cuban soil Columbus spied."

We were passing the Chair of Gibara, jutting alone above the Bay of Bariay in Holguín province. We were heading southeast toward Santiago de Cuba where we would load crude oil. On October 27, 1492, Christopher Columbus and his sailors gazed upon this bay and were the first Europeans to see Cuba. He described the turquoise bay and verdant coastline, which he thought was Japan, this way: "This land is the most beautiful eyes have seen".

Just two weeks before Columbus had "discovered" America when he landed on Guanahaní Island, known today as San Salvador Island, part of the Bahamas. Columbus thought he had found India.

Upon landing in Cuba, Columbus wrote in his log: "I will speak to the King and see if I can get the gold that I hear he wears." The native inhabitants Columbus and his men encountered, the Taínos, called their island Colba—meaning rock, mountain and cave in their language. The Spanish wrote it as Cuba. They came to know it as the Key to the New World. To poets it is the Pearl of the Antilles. The Yankees eventually followed Columbus' greedy quest for gold by making Cuba the Montecarlo of the Caribbean.

Five centuries later, with the commemoration of Columbus' "discovery" still fresh, I was sailing around the independent nation hoping to understand this unique society by inhaling its beauty and dilemmas from the sea. In the course of two years, I made the bojeo and cabotaje (1), and then I sailed on Cuban container ships to Europe and return. In all, I sailed nearly half-a-year. I was the first U.S. citizen to sail on revolutionary Cuba's ships. The only non-Cubans to sail were technical workers from the previous Comecon lands. Cuba has no passenger ships so it took special permission to be aboard tankers and freighters. I worked with the men in order to learn and write about Cuba from the sea.

Bariay's shoreline is nearly barren of life and structures now. There are only a handful of small, rickety houses, mostly summer shacks for fishermen who live in nearby Gibara. A simple plaque marks the spot where Columbus sailed into the narrow bay. I swam in its muddy waters, feeling historically connected.

When I sailed with Sigi, he was already a veteran seaman of 55 years. An erudite man, he loved to read and debate about history and historical figures, such as Columbus.

"Columbus and all his low-breed cohorts were not discoverers of America. They were simply vulgar invaders. America was already inhabited by many peoples, who had migrated from Asia. They had social organizations, economies and cultures. Columbus and his followers were brutal, rapacious invaders. They came with the cross and the sword to plunder in the name of civilization. What they left us—we, who were bred here from their raping and enslavements, such as my forefathers both from Africa and native Americans—is their egoism, ambitions and indifference to others. They left us their social and psychological misery, and half a millennium later this is still affecting our peoples."

I was on watch with Sigi. He had shown me how to steer the helm, and instructed me in the sonar and charting courses, which were beyond my comprehension. Sigi was mostly a self-taught man, who had worked many jobs in his lifetime and fought battles during the revolution, although he never managed to join up with the July 26 Movement. He was always frank with me and a kidder too. On one of several voyages together he told me what he thought of life at sea.

"I've never liked seamanship, though I'm still a merchant marine after 25 years. I got into it because it was a Communist party priority. It was necessary to strengthen our shipping capacity, which was next to nil before the revolutionary triumph. Many compañeros (2) took jobs because the country needed them. We were never made to work where we didn't want to. We were asked and if we agreed then we joined up.

"Well, I learned something new, saw many places and people. The first ship I was shown shocked me it was so huge. I'd never seen a ship up close and didn't care much for it but I launched into this new world from my farming background. After a while, they made me an instructor. Later, the shipping company gave me a task of investigating new recruits. I never went into the merchant marine academy but because of experience at sea, and my own studying, I became an officer. I went through the ranks to pilot, guiding ships in an out of harbor. Today, I have my captain's license but no ship. Continuing as first mate makes no difference to me; it's just a job. I'm no romantic. I love nature but on land. The mountains are what attract me, like la Silla de Gibara, and especially the Sierra Maestra we will soon be passing. I grew up alongside those majestic mountains. The sea is dull in comparison.

"Sure, I can feel some pride in that I'm contributing to the economy, to my country, but I'm only transporting others' sweat. I don't produce anything. I don't sweat. I live a soft life as an officer. It's almost a joy ride sailing around the island, gazing at the shoreline, the sky, the sea. It's not like the deck hands that constantly chip away at the endless rust, or the oilers whose skin is forever greasy black. In my youth, I got more satisfaction as a volunteer doing hard physical labor than in sailing. But I can't regain that sensation by cutting sugar cane for 15 days knowing that I've got such a comfortable life. I make 450 pesos a month basic pay because of my seniority. The first mate basic pay is 310 pesos. But with bonuses for sailing, my monthly income is up to 650 pesos; more than triple the national average wage. But I don't knuckle down like those who cut cane. I just can't feel that pride the sugar cane worker does when he sees a ship filled with sugar, or with crude oil bought with his labor. He can look at this ship and say, `There goes my sweat'."

On hands and knees soaking up water from the uneven deck of his berth is how I first met Captain Miguel Marrón. He wore a frayed T-shirt, baggy Bermuda shorts, and tennis shoes that most youth hanging out on the malecón (3) would not be caught wearing. The captain had curly black hair and sported a bushy black mustache that ended where dimples began on his bulbous, youthful face.

"Welcome. I'll be with you in a moment," he said, wringing out a rag into a bucket. When he stood, a fresh smile spread over full cheeks.

"I'm Captain Miguel Marrón, just mopping up a little leak," he said, sticking out his wet hand to shake. "The second mate forgot to turn off the sink faucet when the pump went out. So when the water flowed again, well, you know, the sink filled up and spilled all over his room and into my berth. The ship leaks a lot anyway. After all, it's 20 years old. She's still running, though. When I get this sopped up, come back and lets talk. The first mate will take you to your quarters. We heard you were coming, quite unusual but you are welcome. How do you pronounce your name?"

"Ron, como en ron." (4)

"No kidding? Hey, we'll have to call him Ron Bocoy, right, first mate."

I would come to drink a lot of this ordinary rum with the captain and Sigi Escalona, who came up smiling at me as he took one of my bags. The captain was smaller than his first mate: too short to make the basketball team, his favorite sport as a youth, and played the guitar instead. Only 33, the captain had already been a seaman for 15 years. The first mate was a generation older.

Sigi led me down the hallway, stepping over puddles on the slatted-hardwood deck.

"Watch your step here," Sigi warned in rapid-fire command speech. "We get leaks sometimes from the boat deck where the swimming pool is. It's only filled when we're in the deep so this leak must originate elsewhere."

He showed me my quarters, the pilot's berth, the size of a jail cell, about 1½ by 2½ meters. There was a narrow bed consisting of a chewed up piece of foam rubber on boards, a chipped sink that didn't work, and a rod with three hangers for clothes. The first mate showed me his spacious two-room cabin and how to operate his tricky shower and toilet.

"You can use my bathroom since your sink doesn't function. Otherwise, you'd have to go down three staircases to use the crew's public showers," he said, handing me an extra key.

Higher ranking officers have two-room cabins with bathroom. Other officers have one room, and non-officers sleep two to a room.

The first mate then took me on a cursory tour of the ship.

The upper bridge is not used for anything other than the telegraph antenna. The lower bridge is a beautiful wooden antique wheel house complete with a hand-cranked magnetic telephone, which makes an authentic ring. The phone is used to communicate with the engine room. A modern telephone hangs on a wall nearby. The wheel house console is made of old hardwood. The helm operates both manually and automatically. There are two radars and a variety of equipment foreign to me.

The boat deck contains the swimming pool just long enough to make three strokes, and gym area with weights and punching bag. Sigi told me that a deckhand is a former world champion boxer. Over the railings hang four life boats.

The two poop decks contain the hospital room, nurse quarters, the purser's berth and many of the crew's cabins. The upper or main deck houses the lowest ranking crew's cabins. These fellows sweat all the time as the engine room is one deck below in the hold where the fuel tanks, water and fuel pumps are also located.

The 9,600-horsepowered engine was built in Poland, a gigantic RD62. The ship weighs 22,000 tons (displacement), carries 16,500 tons of petroleum plus crew (deadweight). At 165 meters long, it is considered a large ship—anything over 145 meters. It measures 21 meters from port to starboard. The Seaweed is one of Cuba's three largest petroleum carriers.

Harry, a balding, stout black man in his late 30s, is the chief engineer. We find him bent over an oily head ring that is four times his weight. They are equally grease black. The engineers and oilers around him appear as dwarfs beside the engine. Whatever their natural skin color, they are all black. Two are greasing bolts one meter long, wise-cracking about sexual organs and slippery entries.

Harry apologized for the dirt.

"You see, we're just finishing repairing the head ring. We lack parts and detergents to properly clean the machinery and us," he laughed.

"The Soviet plant that made these ships doesn't make them anymore and we have to make our own parts. Our most destacado (5) worker is our turner. He sweats over the lathe day and night, making everything from small rings to nuts and bolts and gaskets."

After a four-course hot meal, I explored the decks on my own. I walked on the steel gangway, running the length of the main deck from bridge to forecastle, overlooking a maze of fuel pipelines. The bow stem drew me to the forward drop point just above the sea. All I could see was pitch black liquid. I opened a door under the prow that led down staircases to anchor chains caked in mud. The mud collects when veering in and out and when the water spray system fails to operate the mud cakes. Later, I participated in shoveling mud that was nearly petrified.

Directly underneath the bow stem, beside the anchor room, is the forepeak. It had been used for ballasting but once the ship began carrying only heavy petroleum products, the six-level deep forepart remained unused. Constant erosion from wind and salty sea water seeping in had rusted most of the interior beyond recognition. With a flashlight, I climbed down until I could see the hull bottom. The wall I touched partly pulverized in my fingers. I felt as if the decay would crumble and bury me. The image frightened me. I gained strength upon realizing that three layers of walls separated the forepeak and me from the sea. Nevertheless, it felt like the water would suddenly burst through. I scrambled up the winding staircase, which nearly wedged me in, flung open the hatch and gulped in fresh air.

Benito, the donkeyman, was bent over a fuel pipeline valve. He snapped his head in my direction at the sound of my gasp.

"Hey man, it's close quarters down there!"

"You said it," Benito responded. I hung over a railing while he explained how the tanker is ballasted and bilged.

The Seaweed doesn't have a double-bottomed hull where heavy material can be stored to provide ballast, which produces draft and stability, so sea water is pumped into four of the 21 fuel-carrying tanks, those most corroded and unusable for transporting oil. Ballasting is not permitted until an inspector has determined that no combustible fuel remains in bilge. Sixty tons of residue oil is usually left over after unloading the Seaweed. Every ship has a bilge well where water seepage from the hull's frames collects and is pumped out once the residue oil is siphoned into a well in a balanced manner so that the ship does not tilt. When docked at a refinery, this residue oil bilge is pumped through a hose to a tank where the fuel settles. When the water is basically cleaned of oil it is discharged into the harbor. Benito said this is the major cause of pollution.

The donkeyman took me down into the sweltering fireman's room where he regulates the flow of fuel products by opening and closing wheel valves. The tanks are grouped into fours, each with separate pipes.

"It's absolutely necessary to assure that the tanks are filled evenly for proper keel," he said.

It usually takes 16 hours to fill a tanker with 16,000 tons of crude and 40 hours to unload. Yet it often takes double or more that time due to numerous delays.

Benito led me down into tank no. 1 on the port side. It is 12 meters deep and shaped like a wave so that the product moves easily with the ebb and flow of the ocean. Thick pieces of crust, sediments of oxide, spotted the iron slabs. Tanks must be cleaned with boiling water and washed with a chemical cleaner to prevent sediment crusts from forming and contaminating the product. Indicators show how hot the product is. The temperature should fluctuate between 40 and 62 degrees centigrade depending on the oil's thickness and how much gaseous fumes are present.

I choked from inhaling fumes. Benito said we should have oxygen masks and an indicator if we were to go further down, otherwise we could become asphyxiated. I was relieved when he suggested we should ascend from this black hole. I felt nauseous when he surfaced.

I returned to my quarters to rest and take a swig of rum to rinse out the foul odors. I felt fortunate that I wasn't a donkeyman. Sigi appeared in my doorway. The captain wished to see me in Sigi's administrative office. Representatives from the Havana port authority, from customs and from the shipping company sat around the large oak desk. They handed over 21 copies of the manifesto. Sigi later told me that for many years only three of the 21 copies were needed. He threw the others away. This waste is all the more ridiculous considering that since there are so few copying machines a clerk has to make four sets of carbon copies.

The captain asked where I'd been. When I mentioned the tank I'd just climbed out of it reminded him of a gruesome story.

"I lost a donkeyman not long ago in Nuevitas harbor. A tube was stopped up with gas and he went down to fix the problem. He went into the tank, however, without oxygen equipment. He apparently ignored the alarm that sounded, indicating the fumes were too thick to enable breathing. He continued walking through the passageway at the bottom of the tank. His lungs filled with gas and he conked out. Another seaman realized he was in trouble and descended to help. But he couldn't remain down there without the oxygen apparatus. The men avoid putting it on as it takes time and is a hassle and, in this case, he was in a hurry. The donkeyman died and his colleague nearly did as well. Two seamen put on the oxygen equipment and were able to carry out the second man in time. Luckily, the nurse hadn't gone ashore and she revived him."

We were casting off. I responded joyfully and quickly alongside my new colleagues to the boatswain and second mate's orders, heaving in mooring lines, wrapping the whirling, deadly ropes fast around bitts, cranking in the two 7.5-ton anchors—and we were veering out.

Two small powerful tug boats pushed us out through the harbor. We glided past the Morro Castle and its lighthouse. This stone fortress, located on the eastern corner of the harbor entrance, was in construction for over a century. It was finally finished in the mid-1700s. The Spaniards used it as protection against enemies. The lighthouse sits atop a circular tower 25 meters tall. Its modern light beam rotates every eight minutes and can be seen from 50 nautical miles.

I was exhilarated as we passed by malecón and the tall apartment building where I lived, Edificio Focsa, on the 26th floor.

The engine fell silent as the pilot hopped onto a launch alongside our hull. All ports provide pilots to guide all ships in and out of harbors as a precaution against accidents, at least in Cuba. The captain took over command and sounded three long blasts on the horn. At the sound of the first deafening blast, I ducked and the men laughed. This was the captain's signal to the pilot that we were heading out: course 085 degrees to Matanzas.

I walked across the forecastle and climbed to the bow stem. I faced the vast azure horizon, puffy white clouds and orange-yellow sun. I inhaled fresh wind and listened to the rippling waves the bulb makes with its submarine-like nose just under the surface. Here, there is no ear-piercing human racket, no noxious traffic threatening health and limb. I wished to be that fantasy animal that can live in the sea and on land, under the sea and in the air.

Everything was so new and exciting that I slept little the first evenings. Throughout our voyage, I pitched in on bridge watches, deck maintenance, and assisted with cleaning the engine room. I accompanied the lone donkeyman when unloading at electric plants and cement factories, and loading at refineries. Body discomfitures were soothed by the ever-hypnotizing deep and the swaying vessel.

Seaman's life is mostly maintenance and cleaning. A modern ship is so automated, even these old tankers, that a helmsman is usually not needed when no close to land and when there is little traffic. So helmsmen are assigned to scrape and clean with the deckhands. Even the officers, who conduct four-hour watches, have little to do. They plot courses, making mathematical calculations on charts and making slight bearing adjustments. Not even the captain is necessary most of the time. Of course, the captain is the person to blame when something goes wrong. But his actual duties are limited. Captain Marrón, however, is an energetic man who participated in many tasks. The first mate and the chief engineer are the busy men. The chief's area of responsibility is always in trouble, and the first mate must oversee the boatswain and deckhands, the kitchen and chamber personnel, and the purser. He also takes charge of many financial transactions, receives the manifesto, the supplies, doles out punishments and, along with the captain, grants shore leaves. The captain can intervene at any moment in any area, but rarely does.

I spent a lot of time around Leon on our voyages. The boatswain managed the deckhands, with whom he worked much of the time, and he was my tutor. He took time to explain merchant marine training, work conditions and fleet history.

Cuba hardly had a shipping fleet and no fishing fleet before the revolution. Then, it only had 14 cargo ships—the largest was 7000 tons—and three small tankers which transported molasses. Cuba relied on United States vessels for shipping. In the first five years of revolution, the socialist government bought a score of ships. By the 1990s, it owned 100 general cargo ships, including container vessels, 17 tankers and a couple dozen large fishing vessels that process fish at sea. Cuban waters are home for many varieties of delectable fish and shellfish. Local fishermen catch large quantities of queen lobsters while long distance fishermen bring in the largest quantities of fish for export. Fish products comprise a sizable amount of national income in hard currency. Few natives, however, eat fish. This is both a question of habit and offer. The ministry of internal commerce makes little effort to offer fish to the public. Refrigeration, among other things, is a problem.

Cuba has bought ships not only from the Comecon countries and China but also from Japan, Canada, England, Spain and the Nordic countries. Its tankers are usually limited to transporting petroleum products refined at Havana and Santiago de Cuba to national ports and nearby countries, making the coasting trade. A handful of tankers transport chemical acids and molasses. Most of the ships specialize in transporting one product because cleaning the tanks of crude black petroleum derivatives is costly and time consuming. A few ships carry lighter petroleum products, such as: gas, kerosene and naphtha. The entire fuel fleet has a total capacity of only 100,000 tons, hardly what the largest modern tanker can carry. The former Soviet used to send 300 ships—with a deadweight of 80,000 tons or more—with fuel to Cuba annually, up to 13 millions tons of oil in 1989. A score of Cuban ports receive petroleum products, another score handle general cargo, sugar, cement and minerals. Only a few ports are reserved for fishing and naval usage.

Before the revolution there was no formal education for seamen. Since the 1970s, the usual way to become a seaman is to take the six month course at the Seamen's College, which is open to all over 17 years of age. The training, like all education in Cuba, is free. Here one learns the trade's terminology, how to tie knots, to walk on ship and swim in the sea, how to put out fires and what to do if an accident occurs or if the ship sinks. The student also learns how the ship functions in a broad sense, and then specializes in one of the departments: deck, engine room, donkeyman, kitchen and chambers, and communications. To become a bridge officer, engineer or electrician one has to pass five years of instruction at the Naval Academy. Prerequisites for captaincy conform with universal standards.

General conditions for merchant marines are superior to most all other jobs. Wages are above the national average, from a low of 141 for service workers and 161 pesos for seaman up to 355 for captain (1990s scale). Everyone receives additional bonuses of 5 to 15% when sailing plus extra pay for seniority, hazardous duty, long trips and when work quotas are met. Food is varied, plentiful and free. When traveling abroad warm clothing is provided to all. Every 90 days workers are entitled to 25 days rest plus 10 days vacation. There are complaints, however, that the 90 days sailing time is often extended without consultation. When one's leave is due, the company must provide transportation to return the sailor home.

A nurse of doctor is always aboard cabotaje trips; and always a doctor, usually with a nurse, on long distance voyages. Until the 1990s, ships also employed a politico, a political officer or social-education director. He or she offered information and political briefings to the crew, gave Communist party advice to the captain, and arranged recreation and sports activities.

Tankers provide important services for society but the work is monotonous, risky and stressful. One lives in a potentially dangerous environment. One must always be cautious not to cause fires and explosions, not to solder or produce sharp blows in many places, not to smoke where forbidden. One must be disciplined and calm. Though most sailors do not appear insecure or tense, asthma and hypertension among the most common illnesses treated. Leon was healthy in body and mind, in part, because of his seaman philosophy. A ship is a small town, a world unto itself. If you like that world everything is fine, or at least tolerable; if you don't, then you feel sad and become sick. Leon put it this way: "You must love your ship and the sea. The ship is your house; the captain your father; the crew your family; the sea your world."

Leon was born in a port town, Puerto Padre, in Las Tunas province, in 1944. Raised by his fisherman father, Leon's first job was with the state fishing fleet. Then came military service and fighting counter-revolutionaries in the Escambray mountains. Afterwards, he returned to sea, to tug boats and fishing. But he got tired of the state fishing operation and transferred to dry cargo ships and later to tankers.

Leon joined the Union de Juventud Comunista/UTC (Young Communist League) in 1968, a year after he was promoted to boatswain. In 1974, he joined the Communist party and is now the party's organizing secretary aboard the Seaweed. One third of the crew are CP or UTC members.

"We communists try to help the entire crew develop as workers and persons. We discuss the work and production plans in our party nucleus, and offer our opinions to the ship's leadership. But the ship is run by the captain. Whether he is a member of the party or not, his word is law. The party has no special rights on ships. I ask the captain what his plan is and how the party can help. I never tell him anything. Nor does the party 'spy' on the captain or any sailor. If it did, it wouldn't serve anyone, it wouldn't work. If the captain does something wrong or gives an order that seems incorrect, I might object, but I'll do what he says. If he turns out to be wrong, then I, like any crew member, can accuse him before a company disciplinary hearing.

"We are one big family aboard ship. We take care of each other. We have a routine, a set time to work, to eat, to relax and to sleep. This helps us stay healthy and organized. This way our ship sails smoothly. It is not just a job but a whole way of life. Here, you lose connection with daily events in the streets, in your home on land. But when you see the news on television or hear it on radio, for instance, that a factory did not make its production goals because its fuel was delivered when it should have been, you know you are a vital part of society. You know that many plants and people depend upon your work. It gets in your blood. If it doesn't, you'd better get the hell off the ship."

The life of merchant marines can also be uncertain, Leon adds. One never knows when the job will be done, when the voyage will end or take a new direction. One night stands and longer sexual affairs at various ports can crop up not only for the pleasure of it but as relief from stress. This occurs to women sailors as well, although they must not mention it around men.

The boatswain's blond eyebrows pinched together momentarily and then relaxed.

"I love the motion of the ocean, the solitary life. If I have a problem I take it here and talk to myself. The sea helps me form a life, helps me appreciate my family and friends, helps me meditate, to measure the worth of life. When you think you love or respect someone and you imagine him or her while you are meditating with the ocean's rhythm, you realize if you are lying to yourself or not. When you reach port you are certain what counts and what doesn't."

On course to Matanzas, I picked and hammered at the interminable rust. Sometimes an electric pick hammer was used for the thickest crusts. The perpetual hammering jolted my brain. I had no ear protective device as there were only enough for half the deckhands. Most of the engine crew wore protection; they needed it most.

On hands and knees, we banged and scraped old paint and oxides. We brushed specks with a hard wire brush and then swept the deck clean. We would now rub in oil to prevent dirt from collecting on the deck. Then we would apply the anti-corrosive paint, then two coats of thick paint. When we were about to apply the first coat, seaman Luis took the pail of rust and cast it overboard.

"What are you doing!" I said astonished. "The sea is our mother and you are shitting in her," I continued indignantly.

Startled at my outburst, Luis snorted.

"She's my mother too. But we always throw rust overboard, just like the cook throws garbage overboard, and the entire crew throws their wastes overboard too. What else are we supposed to do with it?"

"You could store it in pails and barrels or special containers, and take it to garbage dumps ashore," I suggested.

"There is no system for that. All the ships would have to have thousands of containers. It would be too difficult and expensive," Luis replied, soberly.

"Well, maybe we lack proper respect for our mother," I moralized. "She is getting sick from all these industrial wastes discarded in her."

"At least we don't throw junk overboard when we're in harbor, not usually anyway," Luis rationalized.

"That doesn't solve the problem. The junk moves anywhere the currents take it, and kills plant and animal life. It contaminates the fish. They get sick and we get sick," I replied.

"Ah, the sea is big; it can hold it all," Luis retorted, petulantly.

Other deckhands listened to us argue, smiling paternalistically at my self-righteous tone. I had stepped out of bounds. Cubans usually avoid biting confrontations.

I shook my head sadly, realizing I could not change their casual notion towards ecology. The entire international maritime industry is contaminated with this listless attitude. Cuba was no different. I stopped lecturing. Luis was sensitive today, anyway. The first mate had just handed him four puestos (6) for failing to return on time from leave in Havana. Luis had checked at the company's operations office to find out when the Seaweed was to sail. Learning that she would depart later than was posted aboard the ship's blackboard, he didn't bother to arrive until she was casting off. He barely made it aboard by jumping from a shuttle launch as she was departing. Sigi did not see the situation the same as had Luis. A captain's orders takes precedence over an operational delay. So Luis must stay aboard ship during the next four port stops. That could mean a month without seeing his wife, or girl friends.

The ship's nurse stood by a railing on the poop deck overhead. I climbed up to speak with her about her job and ecology. The large woman explained that her principle task, besides treatment for minor wounds, was preventive medicine.

"Preventive medicine! Do you think it is healthy for us to routinely dump all sorts of wastes into the sea?" I asked, a bit too forcefully.

She looked at me hesitantly.

"Well," she drawled, "it may not be optimal but its what everybody does all over the world. My job is limited. I look after life aboard ship. I can't worry about the world's ecology. That is for governments to manage. It's chow time; let's eat."

I watched sadly as one more bucket of rust rushed into the sea. A school of dolphins swam past. I doubted that their home is really large enough to harbor them and mankind's garbage.

After chow we approached the new container terminal at Matanzas. A Russian tanker was dwarfed by a 220,000-ton Iraqi tanker. It was so large it could not dock. The Iraqi vessel unloaded its crude directly into tanks of Cuban ships, which would transport the petroleum to Havana's refinery for processing.

Two tugs boats pulled alongside and pushed us to port. I helped deckhands on the bow moor the ship. The heaving line, known as jibalay in pigeon Spanish, is a thin rope with a heavy ball attached to one end. It is thrown lasso style to a dock worker who then pulls it hand over hand until the mooring line reaches a bollard around which he wraps the loop, thus fastening the ship to the dock. On deck, the anchors were dropped and the 80-meter long, steel chains clanged out from the windlass. Deckhands, aft and forward, unwrapped and wrapped lines around bitts and capstans, careful to obtain just the right tension, and the ship gradually swung into its berth. If the tension is too loose, a line could snap during the tightening process and would sling about like lightning. If the rope strikes a person, it will take off that body part it hits. Tremendous energy is required to properly wrap the lines around the cylindrical posts. Men run about in order to keep the proper timing and tension. Many mooring lines are needed to secure a ship: headline, forward breast, forward spring, two abeam, stern line, aft breast and aft spring. I held onto the thick rope with gloved hands and heaved behind three sailors. We fastened double lines around four bitts for extra stability so that the engine could be tested while docked. The last step in mooring is to secure a flat, square piece of rubber or scrap metal over the holes where mooring lines pass through. This prevents rats from scrambling aboard.

Our job completed, we washed, changed clothes and heartily consumed the caldo, malanga, congri, (7) roast pork and sweetened coconut bits. This is a typical meal, although most Cubans in the 1990s were not often able to eat so much. Sailors get two hot meals with meat and two heavy soups, plus two snacks, on a daily basis.

Some men went ashore; others were on watch duty; a few of us gazed at the Russian tanker, which prompted a discussion about the failed perestroika. An oiler made an observation I came to hear often.

"Gorbachev did the work that the entire CIA couldn't accomplish. Gorbachev got his ass greased for Bush's midnight snack and ran out on us. I wouldn't put it past the US government to take advantage of the weak-kneed Russian government to conduct another blockade around us, like what they are doing to Iraq."

Sigi was worried too.

"If perestroika had been applied like it was conceived, and if it had come earlier, it might have been of benefit for socialism, for the Soviet Union and for all socialist countries. But it palled completely. I have often compared what Gorbachev wrote and said with what he did. It didn't match. I think he fooled people so that he could have a free hand to act for capitalism. I've marveled at Gorbachev's ingeniousness. I think he was an agent for imperialism. He said he wanted to eliminate errors made during socialism but he betrayed socialism. He renounced its positive tradition of solidarity with the Third World. He gave the Yankees a free hand to make war in Iraq. He allowed the unification of Germany, and the disappearance of a socialist counterbalance. He even agreed with Bush to withdraw all Soviet troops from out land, thus leaving the Yankee troops on our soil at Guantánamo. It is most disheartening."

On a later short voyage from Las Tunas to Havana—in which I completed the bojeo on the Gold Star—I had a similar conversation with the ship's captain, Humberto Arangueren and the port director, René Marrero.

"The big difference with Cuba and the other previous socialist states is that we began our history by resisting invaders," Marrero said. "Most of the other socialist states did not undergo a revolution and thus did not have a revolutionary conscious people. After our 1959 revolutionary victory, we finally achieved our independence for the first time. And we never gave the Soviet Union one inch of territory, although we became too dependent on them economically, to be sure. But, unlike other supposed socialist states, we remained our own country. Our big mistake was not to take the necessary measures to be self-sufficient in food production. We've begun to do so now. If only we started a generation ago, we'd be sailing smoothly now."

"Why didn't you start a generation ago," I asked.

"It's difficult to know, but no one could foresee then that the socialist world would crumble."

"Perhaps," I said, "but many leftists in the world, and Che, could see that what the Soviets were doing couldn't last. Maybe most Cubans didn't see it coming because there is little debate or criticism in the media and in the educational and political process. Without honest evaluation of facts and divergent ideas, one can't understand reality sufficiently in order to plan ahead intelligently. Moreover, no nation can be truly self-sufficient if it relies on others for its food."

"It's painful to say," Captain Arangueren interjected, "but we became accustomed to what we received so easily from the Soviet Union. We had all we needed, really. It's like father always providing food for his children. They don't worry about getting their own, and you never think about your father dying. But he did. And we weren't prepared. It was a great error, a great error. But I believe the measures we're now taking, including in the maritime industry, will pull us through."

At midnight, I conducted bridge watch with Arturo, the second mate, and Manso, the helmsman. We were on a course of 130 degrees toward Caibarién, the helmsman's home town. Manso grew up in a family of fishermen and merchant marines. His father was a cargo ship captain.

We were passing the Archipiélago de Sabana, one of Cuba's five large bodies of water sprinkled with islets and cays. It runs the entire distance from Matanzas to Caibarién in Santa Clara province.

A star fell over the bow and into a still, flat sea. La mar fuerza cero, (8) declared Manso softly.

A ship was crossing our bow about six miles ahead traveling at our speed, 13.8 knots.

"There's a ship ahead seeming to make circles," Manso informed Arturo, who immediately looked up from checking a chart to study the radar for the ship's bearing, speed and distance from our ship. Six miles separation is the minimum distance considered safe between two ships sailing at perpendicular angles, and the ship passed without any violation of safety rules. Arturo then measured the time lapse between beams emanating from a nearby lighthouse, in order to identify it and thus be certain of our location. He checked the chart and the chronometer to compare our plotted direction with where we actually were in time and space.

"Dead center on course," proclaimed Arturo.

"Sometimes a lighthouse signal is changed," Arturo explained his precaution. "So we must check the international Morse code manual, which is updated regularly, to be certain of signals. If you are wrong about which lighthouse you are passing, you'll not know precisely where you are or what depth the sea is. Accidents happen that way along the coasts."

The second mate was a bookworm. He read constantly and was reputed to be quite knowledgeable about astronomy, the sea and ships, and he kept count of ship wrecks.

"There haven't been many grave accidents despite the vast growth of our fleet. Seven or eight in the first three decades since the revolution. Coral Islands was burnt in port; Arcelio de Iglesia broke in two when it ran into reefs in Asian waters; Pino del Agua was lost at sea; Primero de Mayo sank with a load of cement; Rio Zaza, a fishing boat, collided with another ship. We have men aboard who were on the other two ships that suffered accidents, the San Luis and the 23rd of August. I was the second mate on the 23rd of August. Fortunately, I was off duty at home when it occurred. The third mate had relieved me as a favor. Ravelo was the chief engineer. He's our oiler now. Go talk to him about what happened."

"El mulato del fuego," (9) is scrawled on Ravelo's cabin door.

Ravelo Rodríguez, a tall, slim man of 40 years, was the second ranking officer on the 23rd of August until one day in June of 1989. Like Arturo he was off duty at home when the 4,000-ton Rumanian-built tanker was loading gasoline and kerosene at the Havana refinery. Suddenly, an electric pump exploded in the engine room. The only man on watch duty, an oiler, was burned. He eventually recovered from the wounds. A machinist and the third mate ordered the crew to apply CO_2 to the fire. Someone turned a wrong valve and the fire extinguishers shot the CO_2 over the bow. The fire raged on, approaching the tanks, some of which were filled with gasoline. The crew managed to abandon ship and two tug boats pushed the 23rd of August out of the bay before the fire reached the empty tanks, which exploded and sank the ship. Cuba lost the 8.5 million-ruble vessel and 3000 tons of gasoline. But Cuba was lucky. Had the ship exploded at the refinery, much of Havana would have been lost.

Ravelo and Arturo believe the oiler was at fault because they think he was sleeping rather than inspecting the machinery. The state investigation commission, however, could not determine the actual cause of the explosion. The commission demoted the machinist and third mate for failure to put out the fire. The captain was demoted to helmsman for two years, after which his captaincy was reinstated. Although the captain was ashore, he was blamed for failing to properly train the men in fire control. Arturo said he had conducted several fire drills but they were theoretical ones because there weren't sufficient resources to conduct practical drills. The shipping company also demoted Ravelo to oiler for two years, although it didn't find him culpable for anything connected with the explosion and fire. Administrators said he had violated minor regulations, namely, allowing the engine crew to work six-hour shifts with 12 hours free.

"The 4-hour-on-8-hour-off shift only applies during navigating," Ravelo protested. "Anyway that had nothing to do with the explosion. I feel the sanction is unjust. The authorities simply used me as a scapegoat to take the heat. They couldn't find real causes so they blamed somebody. I think they should have kept on with the investigation."

The next day, I worked with René and other deckhands painting the upper deck. René had been part of the rescue team when the San Luis was split in half near the Bahamas.

"We lost the captain and two inspectors. They were asleep in the captain's berth when a United States passenger ship rammed the San Luis," René told me. "The US vessel had the right of way and it didn't veer as our ship sailed straight ahead in a fog. The captain's berth took a direct hit. Two officers were on the bridge reading charts, and the helmsman was obviously asleep. He lost his legs in the collision. The first mate panicked and jumped overboard without sounding the alarm."

The US shipping company received many millions of dollars in claimed damages. The fact, however, that no one aboard was injured or that the ship had sailed on unperturbed wasn't considered relevant.

"The sea is so immense that it seems boundless," René philosophized. "On longer voyages, it gives you the feeling that you are all alone, that you are just part of the sea. It's then that mistakes occur. When you can see for what seems hundreds of miles and the sea is totally calm, you have a sense of complete security. You get overconfident. The helm can be placed on automatic pilot and the bridge may even be abandoned for a time. Human carelessness is what caused that accident, which was the most serious to any Cuban tanker. Carelessness is a common cause of accidents."

Caibarién fishermen bring in great quantities and varieties of tasty fish, giant turtles, queen lobsters and farmed shrimp. Caibarién is also home of trillions upon trillions of mosquitoes. As we unloaded the rest of our petroleum, swatting at Cuba's most bothersome creatures, I talked with the former featherweight champion of the world, Jesus Sollet Tomacen. I found him on the sports deck lifting weights.

Sollet won the world title in Italy, in 1983, when he was only 21 years old. He retired in 1989. He concluded 16 years of boxing with a record of 391 wins to 28 loses. Sollet had captured Cuba's national featherweight title five times. He won most of his victories fighting international competition in 69 countries. He weighed 57 kilos upon retirement but now the sailor weighed 70 kilos but was still trim and muscular.

"The chow aboard ship agrees with me," he told me, smiling. At 30 years of age, his coal black skin was still baby smooth.

"I grew up on Moa where mining town life can be pretty tough. I got picked on a lot because I was small. My brothers taught me to fight for self defense. I won my first competition fight in Guantánamo city when I was 11 years old."

Sollet went to a physical education oriented secondary school where he studied regular courses and practiced sports. Like all Cuban athletes, Sollet was not a professional but fought in competition while holding his regular job instructing school children in physical education. As a teacher for INDER (10), he was paid 211 pesos monthly to instruct. He earned 120 pesos extra when boxing competition. He quit because he was tired of boxing. Just three years before retirement he had won ten national and world championships. After he won the silver medal at Reno (Nevada) World Cup, he got the offer of a lifetime.

"Reno is eerie. All those bright lights, slot machines clicking, dice rolling, naked dolls slinking about. The whole atmosphere was really weird. And up pops this guy, this 'talent scout' with a signed blank check telling me to name my sum and he'd fill it in. You know, one of those offers 'you can't refuse'.

"I'd heard about this sort of offer but I wasn't thinking about it. This money stuff never tempted me and I didn't hesitate. I never even asked how much. I just shook my head no. He started naming figures in the hundreds of thousands of dollars. If I'd said yes, I could have had a million dollars for only one year of boxing profession in the United States. This guy didn't understand why that amount of money didn't budge me.(11)

"I love what's mine: my family, my country, my Revolution, my comandante. I could never turn my back on my country and that is what accepting such an offer would have meant. I was born here and I'll die here.

"My father was a nickel miner all his life. He brought me up to love our country. When this guy said to me, 'But you could be a millionaire', I responded: 'I am already a millionaire'. Our Revolution made me a millionaire. Millions of Cubans waited for me when I returned from boxing abroad. I am treated as a millionaire with more than money, with the affection of my people."

Sollet fell silent. We strolled over the gangway to the bow. Leaning over the stem, we gazed at the small fishing boats in the harbor. I imagined him in Reno confronted by the All American talent scout, probably fronting for gangsters and/or the CIA. These types think of themselves as real Americans, the kind who shout from the sidelines to "our soldier boys"—plodding through swamps in Asia, trudging over deserts in the Middle East, stumbling through jungles in Latin America—"defending freedom and democracy, the American Way of Life."

La gata, the ship's mouse-eating mascot, slinked up beside Sollet and peered through a mooring line hole. This third generation cat aboard the Seaweed wasn't given a real name. Her mother and grandmother left ship after giving birth to a litter but left one of her kittens for the ship. The men say la gata will do the same. Her favorite amusement is swiping at the mooring lines whirring through the holes as the ship veers in or out. She also likes to swipe at a passing pant leg such as Sollets.

"I love to lean over the bow and stare at the sea," Sollet resumed our conversation. "It's so spell-binding. Seamen's' life is so tranquil. Those Yankees—and I don't mean by that average Americans, just those who aggress against other lands and peoples—just can't understand what it means to love your own country, your own people. I chose sailing cabotage for that reason. I was tired of being away from home. By working tankers I can be home more often, closer to my parents, my wife and three children...and Cuban women. Yes, women are my one vice. I don't drink or smoke but I can't keep my hands off women, especially Cuban women. They are the best lovers in the world."

When Sollet retired from boxing, he was offered a good job teaching physical education at a university of his choice. But he wanted a change. He chose the merchant marines.

"I wanted something entirely new. Maybe I'll return to sports one day but for now I'm happy sailing. I contribute to our fuel needs and the sea is relaxing. What more can a guy want?"

Sollet even earns more money as a sailor than when he was a world boxing champion. His base pay is 300 pesos; with bonuses he often takes home 500 pesos in a month, half as much more than when he boxed. For Sollet that is more money than he needs. And he agrees with the wage system, which rewards productive work more than entertainment or sports activities.

"You see, on ship I am useful, always busy and happy. I party or partake in sports activities when ashore, and I'm active in my union. I am part of a united people, which gives me personal warmth. What can money do for me? Just imagine what my life would have been like had I accepted that million dollar offer. Id be cold and lonely. It's like what Teófilo said—you know, Stevensen, the former world heavy weight champion. He too had been offered a million dollars to fight pro. This was in Munich, and he spoke of it this way:

"If I had all that money, I'd never rest. I'd have to be watching my back all the time, worried somebody was goin' knock me down, maybe kill me, just to get at that money. Now, I have no money in my pockets and no worries."

Caibarién was a short stop. I watched television and read newspapers. One day, Fidel Castro spoke on TV about the current economic crisis and the new plan for survival and recuperation, "The Special Period in Time of Peace."

With the fall of COMECON Cuba had lost 80% of its export income, 63% of its food supplies and 98% of its fuel. Now, the country had to find new buyers for its sugar, nickel, citrus fruits and other bartered goods, and it was forced to initiate cutbacks and seek innovations in the economy. Cutbacks included 50% less gasoline for vehicles, and 30-50% less electricity. Blackouts were conducted alternately in neighborhoods for years to come. Severe rationing of most everything became daily fare for many years. The majority of periodicals were closed or were cut in circulation. Most book publishers were cut to 10% normal output. Two of my books accepted for publication were passed over. I knew of many Cuban authors whose manuscripts were shelved.

The maritime industry was affected like all others. Mambisa took over all tankers and cargo ships. Caribe was limited to running tug boats and flatbed rafts. Cuba began selling some of its broken-down vessels for scrap. All ships' names were changed from Spanish to English ones so that they could more easily be chartered to foreign shippers and get registered in a few foreign countries with minimal restrictions and taxes. By sporting foreign flags, Cuban ships with English names might be able to escape some of the rigors of the United States blockade. Seaweed had been the 9th of April. I would later sail on the 28th of September, renamed Shark. And the Gold Star had been the 7th of November. I would come to sail the Giorita to Holland, which had been the Sierra Maestra. These Spanish names were taken for some significant revolutionary date, place or martyr.

With the advent of hard times came greater insecurity and with it thievery and jineterismo (12). While Cuban sailors have no need of jineteras, some do deal with jineteros and macetas (13) on the black market. Police stepped up vigilance of goods that were disappearing from markets, warehouses and containers transported on ships. In one major maritime scam, in the early 1990s, 42 dock workers, custom inspectors and truck drivers were arrested, tried and sentenced for thievery of eight large containers filled to the brim with imported merchandise. The containers had been lifted from docks onto trucks, who chauffeurs possessed false documents that allowed them to pass through customs. The stolen good were then stored at private farm houses. The underground sale of clothes, shoes, perfumes and cosmetics netted the thieves several hundred thousands pesos and a loss of a million dollars for state enterprises, which would have been realized in dollar shop sales.

Rampant thievery affected seamen's mentality. Donkeyman Benito lamented this turn of events.

"I never used to lock my cabin. We were one solid family aboard ship. Now there is a jinetero element most everywhere you go. They aren't sailors by tradition or love but out of materialistic lust. They are the worst kind of hustlers and thieves. They steal from their own buddies. Everybody has to lock their cabins and hide important possessions now."

Special Period scarcity also resulted in Cuba's inability to buy sufficient parts to repair ships. Variety and quantity of food was more limited for crews, and there were restrictions on overtime pay and travel bonuses, and there was unemployment for the first time in many years. The cost of paints, cleaning chemicals, zinc for tanks, communication equipment, machinery and other necessary items for maintaining a ship became astronomical for Cuba's limited valuta. It now had to buy what it could with precious few dollars, and there were few capitalists who would risk offending the US by selling products to Cuba. When they did, they added a 10 to 20% surcharge for the risk This resulted in postponing repairs and thorough cleaning and painting of vessels. Ships sailing the cabotaje sailed without sonar.

In the early 1990s, Cuba's transport ministry estimated that the US blockade—then 30 years underway—had cost the maritime industry $1.4 billion in losses. An additional $1 billion was lost because the transport industry had to convert to Soviet parts for all the machinery it had originally bought from the US. And now, with the collapse of the Soviet union, it couldn't buy most parts it needed for the COMECON machinery and vessels it had been forced to buy. They had to invent their own. But Cubans are great improvisers. Everyone can see this in how they have maintained with their own ingenuity "good ole American cars" from the time when an automobile was a beaut.

All these shortages and lack of cash caused lengthy dry dock time. Sailors told me that only half the cabotaje tankers were operating normally or at one time. All this caused idleness, restlessness. These conditions influenced some to skip the country. Three captains fled to the U.S. during these hard years. One of them had captained Seaweed just before I sailed with her. He and his wife left their revolutionary daughter behind.

There were some positive aspects to the Special Period. More people were acquiring a sense of self-reliance, fortifying their character and resolve. Hundreds of thousands of city folk volunteered for weeks at a time to till the soil as part of the emergency food production plan. Mysteriously to most of us, however, the fishing and internal commerce ministries did not improve the offer of fish, in fact, it was cut to one small fish per person over a two week period. This caused some young people to create a new black market. They fished with spears off the coasts and sold their catch illegally for many times the normal price.

On the positive front, the maritime industry began using inexpensive flatbed rafts to transport goods locally. The shipwright yard in Santiago de Cuba began building rafts, including ones which could carry combustible fuels. Then it built Cuba's first Ro-ro cargo ship. The roll-on, roll-off vessel allows vehicles and motors to be driven on and off deck, and container cargo can also be accommodated. They are 50 meters long and can carry 500 tons cargo.

The industrial industry invented its own anti-corrosion products to protect ship boilers at a cost of 15% less what Cuba had been paying for imported chemicals. Spare parts technicians built hundreds of fuel emulsifiers to increase energy yield up to ten percent. Many spare parts were being routinely recycled. Cuba also became the first "developing" nation to apply the weather routing system for navigators. Forecasters analyze hydrometerological conditions—the height of waves, the direction and speed of winds—and by using dead reckoning estimates determine the location of ships and where they will be in hours or days. Captains use this information to make educated guesses at what the weather will be like further ahead in a day or so, thus enabling them to choose the shortest or safest routes. In the first years of usage, the weather routing system saved Cuba thousands of tons of fuel, thousands of hours in navigating time and money.

Cuba is also using its own heavy crude oil, thus replacing some imported diesel oil. In the early 1990s, Cuba was extracting one million tons of crude oil from its soil and shorefronts. Canadian and Italian oil companies were contracted to search for more and better quality oil. A decade later, it looked like Cuba might one day be able to be self-sufficient in oil recently found.

With the merger of the two shipping lines, experienced ship captains took administration jobs and thousands of administrators, technocrats and office workers were weeded out. Many were place in productive jobs, including farm work, others went into retirement (55 for women, 60 for men). Cost accountability was now the modus operendi.

As we sailed from Caibarién to Santiago de Cuba, in order to reload with petroleum, I worked in the engine room. Once reloaded, we would navigate the southern coast delivering crude to Cienfuegos and Mariel before returning to Havana for a rest. During this time, I attended meetings concerning production and atención al hombre (14), as well as a unique assembly to discuss the Communist party's fourth congress call.

Working in the engine room takes the steam out of you. The temperature is 60 degrees beside a cylinder. It took an entire morning to clean the seven-ton cylinder, which is taller than me. Later, I assisted in positioning one of the six pistons in the block. This was all new and exciting work for me. Of course, I cleaned old and crusted pipes and tubes, which sometimes burst under pressure and break into pieces. I was present when a tube busted and the boiler had to be shut off. The accumulation of chemicals from the constant circulation of fresh and sea waters created blockages of crusts. It took us all day and night to temporarily fix the pipe by blocking circulation, thereby delaying the loading process. We'd have to replace the tube in Havana.

After one day shift, engineers and oilers met to discuss who should be chosen destacado, and a discipline problem. A man had failed to observe an equipment check. He admitted his negligence and was admonished. The chief engineer restricted him to ship for the next two port stops. Everyone was urged to attend the production and service assembly later.

I showered and dove into the three-meter deep pool. After chow, most of us gathered in the mess hall for the meeting. We heard a report that the recent volunteer day "inspired too little enthusiasm." Sigi had been the only volunteer to scrape rust. Deckhands were not about to volunteer to scrape even more rust. But five crewmen had cleaned rice and empty bottles. The empties would be returned to Havana and recycled. The 20 centavos per bottle earned would go to sports and union activities.

The men were berated for being too lax in saving energy. Almost nobody thinks about turning off lights when leaving a room. Water would henceforth be turned on only three times daily for one to two hours.

The first mate took the floor to read results of the last quarter. Seaweed had made ten production trips of the 13 planned, delivering 156,000 tons of petroleum instead of the 205,000 goal, and earned 600,000 pesos instead of the 970,000 hoped for. Monetary intake was simply paper notations as far as the shipping company was concerned, however. All financial matters went through JUCEPLAN (15), which, along with ministries, decided what money exchanges were made. In the near future, this process would be changed to a cost accountability one with each production center, or vessel, having to make ends meet.

Chief engineer Harry pointed out that the ship had been out of commission 13 days due to repairs in dock. During a 30 day period, his crew had made 14 repairs on the engine, boiler, fuel line, lights and lifeboats.

I was pleased to hear several men speak up when the floor was opened for general discussion. Such participation had been lacking where I worked at José Martí publishing house. Several men complained about one thing or another yet offered no solutions. The few women attending remained silent. Irritations were expressed about the lack of juice and soap, and the distribution of beer. Some had not received their share of the limited juice because after night shift they were asleep when the cans were passed out. The captain said that each gets the same quantity and if one is not present during distribution then his quota is saved. The matter ended there, although the captain had merely stated policy without responding to what actually occurs.

Oilers objected to having to eat standing up on deck because they don't have time to clean up while working and thus can not sit in the mess hall. There wasn't enough detergent either, and the limited Cuban brand is not strong enough to do an adequate job. Captain Marrón suggested, it seemed in irony, that the officers donate half their ration to the engine room. The men rejected the offer out of hand, because, I thought, they would feel humiliated. No other solution was offered.

Everyone was aware that there were 30 cases of beer aboard and anticipated that some would be passed out following the meeting. The beer question was related to the juice matter because some men don't always get a full share, which is usually two bottles at any serving. The captain asserted that he would maintain the same policy—passing out beer based on availability and his timing instinct—because to pass out an entire month's ration at one time would result in intoxication, hoarding and selling.

The captain and union steward reported that they had complained "through the proper channels about the lack of bedclothes". There was grumbling but nothing was stated. Afterwards, I was told that this union steward had been sent to the ship by the party and union hierarchy. The previous representative, who had been selected by the crew, had been too "outspoken".

A new sports program was announced for the coming month. Sollet would help arrange tournaments of dominoes, chess and ping pong. Arturo later won, leaving me in second place.

The purser concluded the meeting by announcing that he would now sell the cigarette quota at the regular price, 30 centavos a pack, and regretted that there hadn't been as much food as usual. I simply couldn't eat all that was served.

BEER TIME! Cold "Tropical". It sure tastes good, especially after a sweltering day in the boiler room. It would taste even better if drunk just after the shift when sweating profusely, but it is understandable that there must be control and limited intake when sailing a vessel. Besides, it is given free and few other workers get beer on the job.

I awoke before dawn and hurried to the bridge to witness the historic landmark, Bariay. I stood beside Sigi at the helm as the sun dawned and we could see where Columbus first disembarked in Cuba. Throughout most of the day I gazed at the beautiful shoreline. It was a sunny day and I was enraptured at the lush foliage along the shore. At mid-day we passed slowly before Yunque de Baracoa.(16) This 530-meter high, odd-shaped mountain standing alone was sighted by Columbus on November 27, 1492. He disembarked here and spent a good deal of time enthralled with the beauty of nature and friendliness of the natives. In 1512, Diego Velázquez came to slaughter the people and force the captured to build the first Spanish settlement at Baracoa. It was here around the easternmost tip of Cuba at Punta de Quemado that Columbus witnessed the most precious of scenery "eyes have seen".

I was fortunate not to have to work set hours and took advantage of this day to take in the landscape from the bridge, bow and stern. It was a time to contemplate nature and mankind's development these past five centuries. I also contemplated at what I had witnessed in my lifetime, from the advent of television to war as a permanent point of reference. And here I was defying the war-makers by enjoying the company of a people just as friendly and open as were the Taínos when they embraced their soon-to-be murderers. The film, "The Mission", captured this dichotomy. It is as though the natives were, just like the Cubans, too good with one another to be allowed to live by a people raised to be bad with one another. I came to think of the time I was in the jingoists' Air Force. I never witnessed the fraternity that exists here among officers and men. Under Captain Marrón vibrations among the crew were smooth and cheerful. His door, and the first mate's, was always open. It was common for officers and men to be found in the captain's berth watching television or a video, smoking and sometimes drinking beer—although never to the point of intoxication. The captain did not appear any different than the rest of the crew. His speech was that of the street and I never once saw him in uniform. He was just as often interrupted during conversations as any seaman.

After chow, I found the captain watching television in his cabin. He invited me in for a beer.

"Tomorrow a party representative from Havana will board ship and help conduct the afternoon meeting. It will be good for you to partake," the captain told me.

"Great. Can I say what I want?"

"Sure," he replied unhesitatingly, and then paused before continuing. "Of course, you know the difference between `All within the Revolution, nothing against it'? The party will not discuss multiparty systems, capitalist measures, or direct vote for the presidency."

"Yes. I know. But, for instance, could I say that I think it was a good idea that you suggested the officers could donate half their soap ration to the crew. It is the men who get greasy not the officers. That would be practicing camaraderie and egalitarianism."

"Oh, Ron, you are a romantic idealist," he laughed. "Anyway, don't worry about it. I've solved the problem. I told the purser to release some of our soap reserves, which we keep—among other items—for just such an occasion as this one."

That seemed rather cynical to me, that there is a policy to dole out a little extra here and there when the men complain loudly. And it borders on lying to the men when they are so often told no hay (17). I felt disappointed and excited, open to new experiences at Santiago de Cuba.

Cuba has no nationality divisions or separate cultures. Despite this unity, there is a certain regional rivalry, mostly fun loving. It is said that naquitos (18) are the most laid back of all Cubans and the "hottest" due to the more humid, hot climate and their hot sensuality. The aseres (19) are said to be arrogant and not as hospitable as other Cubans. Although naquitos contend they don't like Havana, half of them migrated to Havana following the revolutionary triumph. When taunted about this by aseres, Santiagans retort that since half the Havanans fled the fatherland for Miami consumerism and counterrevolutionary ideology the easterners had to populate the capital city.

Some of the inter-provincial kidding stems from differences of dialect. Easterners "sing" more than westerners, much like other Caribbean islanders and Central Americans. Intonations and pitches are higher, especially at the end of sentences. They leave out "s" sounds altogether at the end of words, as do the French and Andulacians. Many of the latter migrated to eastern Cuba. Easterners are rhythmically more "Latin" due, in part, to African influences. Havanas speak more evenly and flatly. All Cubans speak rapidly, many mumble whole syllables, but easterners speak even more rapidly. They also dance faster, and their body movements and hand gestures are most exaggerated.

Many of these characteristics were noticeable among the merchant marines I sailed with. There was no end of aseres ribbing naquitos and vice versa. This became more evident when we arrived in Santiago de Cuba. But once ashore, the naquitos took care of their compañero aseres. Before we could partake of the city's delights, however, we participated in the workers' assembly.

Perhaps because of the recent fall of the Soviet Union and Comecon, the Cuban Communist party took greater care of the entire people by inviting everyone to participate in discussing party policy. Members and non-members alike were encouraged to meet in their local neighborhoods and work centers to discuss the food plan, the process known as rectification of errors, the popular power and party organizations, and other matters of major concern. People were asked to make suggestions to improve the socialist system, the only one remaining in the western hemisphere. In the call for the 4th congress, party leadership acknowledged deficiencies and criticized itself for errors. It stated that the party had created an "unreal image of unanimity", one which is often "false, mechanical and formalistic". The party must give space to "diversity of criteria", and the media must "continue propitiating a climate of openness (become) more profound, analytical and critical", in order to advance "the knowledge and participation of the people in all fronts of the Revolution".

Many people did not believe that the party leadership actually meant what they said and few non-members entered into the requested dialogue. Their experience led them to believe that the party did not truly want to hear criticisms or new ideas. The public meetings were suspended and discussion returned inwardly with television coverage. Once the public saw that party members were speaking out more openly than customary, then non-members were more prepared to discuss the party document. Eventually, 80,000 assemblies were held and one million complaints and proposals were noted, computerized and processed by a congressional commission. Some of them were taken up and decided upon at the 4th congress.

The party's representative from Havana related some of this background to the seamen's assembly. She was accompanied at the presidium by the ship's party secretary, Leon, and a political officer. About half the crew participated. Others were on duty or uninterested.

The union steward opened the discussion by criticizing the shipping company's "poor coordination, which causes fuel wastes and unnecessary delays". Captain Marrón responded that the discussion should be held about "larger issues and not on details". A machinist challenged the captain's intervention. "Anyone should say what he wishes bit it a `detail' or not. The captain and other officers should not feel that they must respond to every person or lead the discussion." The captain remained silent.

Although the meeting was directed in a stiff manner, several men, like the machinist, livened it up. A helmsman suggested, for instance, that Cuba should develop "its own economy and not rely on others, nor offer so much assistance to others".

Sigi participated quite sharply.

"We live with slogans as part of our diet. `Save' is now in vogue. But we don't internalize the real need to save energy, to turn off unused lights, shut off water valves. Why not? Because we know that the leadership takes us on one marathon after another without ever reaching the goal. There is too little true analysis of structures, methods, results. True incentives to take initiative, to be creative, must be developed and popularized so that we can construct a real socialist democracy. The government opens doors, for instance, for foreign capitalism. Why not for us?"

Sigi did not offer any concrete proposals, and no one engaged him in a deep analysis, but his was a welcomed commentary by all. This was a rarity in itself. Men nodded and gestured approvingly.

Several comments were directed at the union—seen as a Communist party facade. Leadership is appointed by party leaders and not voted on by workers. The captain said that some local unions were beginning to elect their immediate representatives. He defended the way "socialist unions" are as "necessarily supportive of our administrators. We are the owners. In capitalism, for instance, strikes must be used to curtail the ruling class' interests, but not here, not in socialism."

No one disagreed but those who spoke up wanted their unions to have more power. "The captain, for example, can forbid our union representative from leaving ship to try to resolve a problem for us," protested one seaman. Even Leon was critical: "Union functionaries and representatives have all too often little interest in real union matters. But the workers are to blame as well."

I spoke about the role of the media in promoting a workers democratic socialist state, and contended that the media was neither professional or fulfilling its constitutionally codified role of representing the people.

"The people are not heard in the media. There are no opinion pages, debates or letters-to-the-editor. And the man-on-the-street quotations are not comprehensive. All we get is hip hip hurrah unanimity. I propose that this assembly adopt a motion calling upon the party, which controls the media, to implement concrete steps to open the media by starting with such public input."

The chairwoman ruled my motion out of order as it "is not in the area of seamanship issues. Furthermore, the government is under attack by the foreign media and this is a touchy theme."

I objected. "We have already discussed areas not related to the maritime industry. Furthermore, the Cuban constitution clearly states that the media is everyone's concern."

There was huddle at the presidium, and the chair relented. My motion could be discussed.

Sigi supported my motion.

"The party must cease controlling and monopolizing the media. The people don't have power, neither in the media or in their mass organizations and `popular power' government."

My motion passed unanimously. So did Sigi's subsequent proposal calling for "democratizing the mass organizations and popular power government, conduct real elections and elect young people and women".

The meeting adjourned with the promise that our discussion and two motions would be computerized and sent to the congress.

I asked several for their evaluations of the assembly. The consensus was: "Words and motions are meaningless. Nothing will come of it. Empty rhetoric." Some men did concede that this was more open than most meetings.

Afterwards I went to the captain's cabin. He was drinking a beer alone.

"Hey Ron, I'm glad you're here. Come in and have a beer."

I walked to the refrigerator and took out a "Tropical" bottled beer. I asked what he thought of the assembly.

"You know, Ron, I've been meaning to tell you something and now is a good time. I carry my heart in my hands. I am concerned that we are always talking politics, world problems. You are a man of the world, the political world, a traveler. I am a simple man. I prefer to dedicate myself to my work. Oftentimes, I don't even read the newspaper. When you came aboard, I thought: what is this, an American, a journalist, an American journalist on my ship. What does he think? What does he want? Now, I look at you as a brother. You are much more than a journalist, than an American. You participate with us. You live like a Cuban. I admire you, Ron. But I must say that I am tired of discussing political problems, economic problems, contradictions within socialism. I want to know you as a brother. I want to share chicks and booze with you. I want to be your friend, not just an object of your work—a seaman, a Communist. Do you understand?" Captain Marrón was serious. I appreciated his honesty, his sentiments. We would soon put his desire into action but before that Sigi gave me his views of his brethren, Cuba's culture.

SIGI talks about the Cuban people

Cuba is a country of mixed bloods, predominately mulato, like me. We've got Indian, Spanish, French, English, Chinese, African in us. Although my appearance is mulato, I identify mostly with aborigine people. There are still a few descendents in the east, and in my family there are some Indian features. My oldest son looks typically Indian with longer, softer black hair and copper-colored skin. My grandfather on my mother's side was mulato. He was a captain during the war for independence. His wife was Spanish from the Canary Island, typically blond and white-skinned. On my other side, they were mostly mulato.

A Cuban is first and foremost amiable, joyful, always in love or soon to be, and caring affectionately for those in his life. He is also jodedor, parrandero, bullanquero, arriesgado, guapo. [joker, clownish; merry, reveller; boisterous, loud-mouthed; daring; bold, handsome.]

When possible he is non-violent, but beware not to ruffle a Cuban's dignity for he'll become fierce. It is not by coincidence that we produce the world's greatest boxers.

Cubans like to criticize but can't stand to be criticized. Cubans are dignified, decorous, honorable. A Cuban likes to serve those close to him but dislikes being a servant or waiter. He can be quite toilsome when motivated. Cubans are proud and pretentious. They love to dress up in fine clothes, to eat well and plentifully, to drink lots of rum and makes lots of love. Men are womanizers; women are flirtatious.

Cubans are not avaricious and like to share what they have with friends and even new acquaintances. They accept whatever responsibility and dangerous situation without concern for their safety, especially in the most critical, dangerous moments. In times of crises, Cubans do not lose their sense of humor and animation.

A Cuban is clearly distinctive in a group of non-Cubans. You notice him by his sense of joy, affability, boisterousness, and rapid speech. The Cuban language is an argot unto itself and Cubans are garrulous, and exaggerate the truth.

Cubans are solidary at heart, internationalist by ideology, sensitive to injustice and will not tolerate abuse. One of the pillars of our revolution is our sense of brotherhood with the oppressed of the world. We have long offered solidarity in all forms to people and some brother governments when under attack by foreign powers or when nature destroys. We are Spartan against the enemy and humanitarian towards the people of the world. We feel some bitterness now that so many governments we've helped have turned their backs on us, or have crumbled. Still, I am proud of how we've behaved in world affairs. We are pleased to see so many thousands of foreign youngsters studying here, and those who get medical care, and all free. Still, I think we should be more careful about where we send aid. Today, many Cubans go on international missions to buy what they can. Egoism reigns.

Notes:

(1) Bojeo means sailing around the entire island-nation, which is 1,456 nautical miles. Cabotaje means the coasting trade in and nearby Cuba.

(2) Friend or partner. In revolutionary Cuba, the entire people who support the process are compañeros.

(3) The long concrete seawall in Havana where romance and strolling are common.

(4) Ron means rum in Spanish and is not a personal name in that language.

(5) Distinguished, vanguard.

(6) Demerits.

(7) Caldo=thick meat broth with vegetables; malanga=farinacious root; congri or moros y cristianos= beans and rice or Moors and Christians.

(8) The sea is force zero. Spanish speaking sailors use the feminine gender for sea, stemming from the Greeks and Africans, who believed that the sea is our mother, that all life springs from the ocean and thus mankind dates back to her. Zero force stands for total calm on the Beaufort Wind Scale, which is the seaman's scale classifying wind velocity and storm descriptions. Beaufort was a British admiral who devised the scale in the early 19th century. A gale or cyclone begins at force 8 (34 to 40-knot winds with waves of 4-6 meter heights), and a hurricane at 12 (64+knot winds with waves of 14+ meters).

(9) The mulatto of the fire.

(10) Instituto Nacional de Deporte y Recreación (National Institute of Sport and Recreation).

(11) See my book, Backfire: The CIA's Biggest Burn (Editorial José Martí, Havana, 1991) pages 150-2, for an explanation of why the CIA underestimates Cubans.

(12) Socialist Cuba's special brand of exchanging sex for foreign goods or just a good time on the town. Jineteras are often college students. Later, when the tourist trade really caught on regular prostitution set in with the exchange of sex for dollars.

(13) Jineteros are males who hustle women, or steal and sell black market items to machetas, who are fences with capital.

(14) Providing decent working conditions and service to workers.

(15) Junta Central de Planificación/Central Planning Board.

(16) Baracoa Anvil, shaped like a square-top anvil.

(17) There is none.

(18) Natives of Santiago de Cuba, a term they affectionately apply to themselves.

(19) Natives of Havana, literally meaning human beings.

CHAPTER TWO: PORT SANTIAGO DE CUBA

Figure 6: Ron working on "Seaweed", Cuba, 1991.

The new hydraulic fuel pump line sprang a leak. As soon as it was fixed a valve busted. A dock worker at the refinery said the only man who had parts and skill to repair it had left.

"We'll be stuck here until Monday before it's fixed," said Benito, grinning. "You think they'll find their men over the weekend? Forget it. This is Santiago de Cuba, another republic with its own rules, with the worst bureaucracy and the most fun-loving people. Let's go party."

Friendship ties, personal sentiments, momentary moods play the decisive role in interrelations in this supreme Caribbean city. This meant we would spend four days before we could reload with petroleum, time enough to explore this picturesque setting and to party.

The coastline is dotted with old wooden houses, fishermen in rowboats and several small restaurants. Sierra Masestra hillsides surround Cuba's second largest city of 350,000 inhabitants. Santiago is known as the "Hero City of the Revolution" because of important struggles waged by its residents for independence from Spain and later for the revolution against the Batista-Mafia government. The Fidel-led guerrillas had their main base in the surrounding mountains, and it was here that Fidel entered in victory in the first days of January 1959 while Che and Camilo led their guerrilla brigades to victory in Santa Clara and then to Havana on New Years Day.

Santiago de Cuba was the first capital city, which Diego de Velázquez had built in 1514. Havana was designated the nation's capital in 1553. To the east lays Cuba's largest national park, Baconão, where the Gran Piedra (1) area served as hideout for native "Indians" and cimarrones (2), who escaped Spanish conquistadores and slavers. The Gran Piedra was later used for the same purpose by Cubans fighting for independence from Spain, the Mambisas, and later the 26 of July guerrillas.

The humid mountainsides and surrounding fields provide rich soil for banana plantations, cocoa and coffee. French landowners, who fled their black slaves in Haiti following successful uprisings 1791-4, set up coffee plantations here. The Spanish overlords built the beautiful Morro Castle as a prison and to protect them from pirates, among them the formidable Englishman Henry Morgan. On top of El Cobre copper mine stands Cuba's most adored Catholic church where Afro-Cuban Santaría worshippers also pray.

Only one small café remains on the waterfront, El Farito. It sometimes served beer with its one meal. The place was packed. Around the eight tables stood dozens of men and women waiting to sit; some were already eating standing up. No menu was necessary. The only meal served consisted of pork chops and rice and beans. One glassy-eyed man wavered by the cash register, devouring his thick pork chop with his fingers, fat smeared across his lips and cheeks. I had no patience to wait so I walked through Alameda barrio where dilapidated wooden houses were barely supported by shaky posts and crumbling bricks. The narrow uphill streets reminded me of San Francisco. One street was lined with people standing and sitting on the sidewalk waiting to buy kerosene for cooking. One old man clutched a large tin can once used to contain cooking oil. He told me they had been waiting two hours and the attendant hadn't yet begun serving.

At the top of Heredia Street is Cespedes Park, the central square with its lovely trees and benches. Former colonializer homes, such as Velázquez', had been turned into museums, hotels and the chess academy. The latter was filled with men quietly concentrating on their matches. At Hotel Casa Grande only half the restaurant tables were being served. Although there was a long line of people snaked around the sidewalk waiting for a table, the other half was closed off and the bar was closed. Rum and beer quotas were sold out. Reservations for a table were no longer being taken even though it wasn't yet dark. There simply wasn't enough food.

Although Santiago de Cuba is famous for distilling the nation's best rums—Havana Club, Matusalém and Caney (the former Bacardi) and beer—Hatuey—none were to be found. I walked up and down main streets and side streets. No rum. No beer. I couldn't even find paper or notebooks I needed for note taking. Shopkeepers said they'd not be restocked for months. School children get paper delivered to the schools. At the office of the Union for Writers and Artists, the director gave me a few sheets of paper. Finally, I found a place with excellent ice cream. Cuba makes as rich and tasty ice cream as can be found anywhere in the world. Service was even slower than in Havana, but when the ice cream came it came with a smile and a glass of precious water, and promise of a refill.

Fortified, I continued my explorations. The city's architecture is a fascinating conglomerate of Roman, Greek, Baroque, Arabic, Renaissance and Chalet styles. Stately stone, smooth hard wood, bright red tile and wrought iron dominated the city. Like Old Havana, much of the city's elegance was deteriorating. However some of the city had recently received a partial face lift and new developments had been constructed as part of the Communist party fourth congress celebration, which took place in the Hero city. Among the many redevelopment projects was the construction of four hospitals, 818 new family doctor clinic-home apartments, the modernization of the oil refinery as well as many industrial works and agricultural expansion. Several hotels, including a luxurious 5-star one, were being built or had been just built, in order to expand the tourist trade, which would soon become the nation's number one source of hard currency. Two of the new hotels had been built for the 1991 Pan American Games as part of an entire sports village with five sports stadiums. All of Cuba vibrates to musical sounds of mixed genres emanating from its hybrid populations. In recognition of the son and the salsa, largely inspired by the mainly black population, the city built the nation's second Tropicana Cabaret in 1991. Santiago is also noted for the Caribbean Folk Music Festival and the popular hip-grinding, congo-drumming Carnival. The nation's most modern and attractive theater, Heredia, was also built in this period as was an artistic statute of the liberation hero Antonio Maceo. The Hero city was successfully fighting against stark economic losses and showing the way to redevelopment, all within the context of food and beverage shortages.

After wandering about the hot city for several hours, I ran into deckhands Carlos and Lazaro on the prowl. Carlos hailed from here. He must know where to quench our thirst. If we could find booze women would present themselves. We passed through central park where people were eyeing tourists bearing bottles of the best rums, yet I detected no hostility—only flickers of envy. Carlos led us to the Lenin Hotel. He was certain we'd find something there. The grounds were magnificent. The green lawn was covered with dozens of varieties of flowers, plants and magnificent trees: ceiba, flamboyant, oak, poplar, mahogony and the omnipresent Royal Palm. So inviting, yet so closed. I counted 20 entrance doors to the large building and more doors inside the salons, restaurants and bars. Seventeen of the entrance doors were locked and three portals were half opened. The bars were locked despite signs posted indicating they should be operating. Restaurants doors were half closed and service had stopped. No hay!

My throat was parched. Asere Lazaro looked drawn; Naquito Carlos looked optimistic. He led us back to the wharf. where we hit pay dirt. El Farito was open and the queue wasn't long. An hour later, we sat down to pork chops, rice, malanga, and the two beer limit. Sabores ENSA was a new beer to me. Carlos explained that it had been specifically concocted and brewed here for export to Angola but the deal fell through and so the beer was placed on the Cuban market, mainly in this region. It had a fine pilsner flavor.

As darkness fell, we milled about the waterfront waiting for the rest of the crew to come ashore and for Nautico, the open-air cabaret, to open. Soon, we saw Captain Marrón with other officers and crewmen stepping ashore from the early evening launch. We hailed each other warmly and with light hearts walked down to Nautico.

Socially necessary modes of conduct in the interest of mutual survival are generally respected by most Cubans. In comparison to world averages, especially for poor countries, criminality has not been a large problem for most of the time since the 1959 revolution. In the early years of the special period thievery did increase significantly, but major crime, organized crime with mafias, or street gangs terrorizing neighborhoods did not set in. Murders and rapes were still not common. Besides laws against criminality, government institutions and the Communist party make many rules and formalities. Many of these are routinely ignored and ways around them are invented. Violators do not fear reprisals. What I saw at the night club is a common example of this. Authorities had imposed "the rule of pairs" as requirement for night club entry in the social interest of preventing jealousy and envy from flaring into violent conflicts. While this limits individual freedom, the object is to avoid fights over a single woman. Once inside the clubs, "couples" are free to part and dance with anyone he or she pleases.

Outside the cabaret, single men and single women milled about; some almost lined up looking for someone to pair with. This occurred in full view of club leaders and police. No one seemed bothered. There were a few pairs already in line waiting for the doors to open but most were singles and singles in groups eyeing each other to see whom would approach whom. The women stood or sat calmly confident they would find a suitable acquaintance or stranger to escort them inside.

Our crew split into three groups. I was with Lazaro, Carlos, Guillermo and Tómas. We picked up four morenas (3). A few minutes after the cabaret opened all the seamen had found pro forma partners. The entrance fee was symbolic. We were lucky to get a table not far from the counter bar. The stage was set with the sea in the background. We men got up to buy our limit of one bottle of rum per person. To our pleasant surprise they were selling my namesake, Ron Paticruzada, the sailor rum because a seaman is on the label with his legs crossed. This is either a sexual message or a joke, since sailors never have their legs crossed while sailing. And they even had ice. We drank the good rum straight or on the rocks, perhaps with lime, which the girls had brought. We danced until our clothes were dripping wet. "My" girl was unusually timid but the rest of the women and sailors at our table made up for her occasional coquettish whisperings. Loud laughter, boisterous conversation, and gesticulating hands and arms permeated the starlit atmosphere. The place was packed with hundreds of local folk and sailors shouting, gulping down rum, dancing dry-humping style. I danced with different women close to the stage where long-legged, half-nude showgirls wriggled their stuff.

This was my first night out with seamen and I wanted to get drunk and laid. Although my "date" warmed up to me as we grinded on the dance floor, I wasn't in the mood to scurry about to find a place to fuck. We couldn't go to her place because she lived with a family of eight in a two-room shack. The few posadas (4) would certainly be full this weekend night.

I walked over to the captain's table and we cheerfully raised glasses. Some of the men were dancing, others were chatting. I sat down. We spoke about nothing in particular and drank. I had to piss but didn't want to enter the putrid toilet, an open area simply screened off with slabs of high boards where one urinated or defecated on the concrete floor. I picked up my bottle, down to three-finger level, and maneuvered my way outside the cabaret to find a tree. Finding none, I bent over the wire fence enclosing the club and pissed on a patch of weeds while holding the bottle behind my back with my free hand. Suddenly I felt a jerk from behind and turned around unsteadily, my penis still dripping, and watched two teenagers run away with my bottle. I was too far gone to chase after them. When I got back to my table, some of the men were waiting for me to return to ship. The last launch was about to leave. But I wanted more to drink. Tómas said he'd take care of me. We drank the last of his rum while my "date" stroked my leg.

When I awoke, I didn't have the faintest idea where I was. All I could remember was someone repeating, "Chico, ven, ven comigo" (5). My head was splitting and the radio news did not make it better. I slowly raised my swollen head and gazed about. I was in a windowless room, which looked like a rundown, barren boarding house without beds. I was sitting in a small, synthetic covered chair. Besides me was a wooden staircase down which came an elderly black woman. She smiled, said good morning and put a cup of coffee in front of me. She then returned up the stairs. I drank the very sweet, luke-warm coffee and wobbled up the stairs where there was a tiny two-room apartment. Tómas was stretched out on the only bed. The woman bent over him shaking his leaden body.

"Son, get up. The launch will be leaving soon."

Tómas managed to crawl off the bed, gulp down coffee, brush his teeth, and out the door we zigzagged toward the quay. Captain Marrón and Sigi ribbed me about my hangover and that I'd been vulnerable enough to allow two squirts to steal my cane juice. I didn't return to town anymore. I decided to spend the remaining days working aboard ship—sort of a self-made penance.

Notes:

1. Great Rock
2. Runaway slaves who lived in the wilds.
3. Brown or mulata girls.
4. "Love hotels" run by the state where one pays a small rental fee for a room by the hour.
5. "Kid, come, come with me."

CHAPTER THREE: PORT CIENFUEGOS

It took a full day and night navigating from Santiago de Cuba over halfway up the western coast to Cienfuegos, some 250 nautical miles. We passed the serene Sierra Maestra range, rounded rocky Cabo Cruz and sailed alongside Camagüey's cattle country.

The province of Cienfuegos is noted for its abundance of sugarcane, fine cigar tobacco and fruits. In the northern part lays Escambray mountains where Cuban counter-revolutionaries—former supporters of the dictatorship and some other disgruntled residents in Cuba and Cuban exile infiltrators from Miami—staged the fiercest battles against the young revolutionary government. The CIA conducted Kennedy's presidential plan, Operation Mongoose, to overthrow the government and reinstate U.S. economic and political dominance. This aggression, as all the many criminal covert and overt military actions, failed.

Cienfuegos' is one of the deepest and busiest ports in Cuba, and a major trading town. We neared the long harbor's narrow mouth in the darkness. It took several hours for the pilot to come aboard and guide us. Large ships can not dock at the quay because it is too small. Large vessels must anchor at buoys. Thick rubber and steel hose lines are connected underwater to the ships' tanks and the receiving electric and fertilizer plants. To avoid accidents, such as hoses breaking and subsequent pollution of the waters and fauna, divers must check the hoses while ships load and unload petroleum products.

Mooring eight lines to four floating buoys is not easy. Two tug boats pushed us back and forth, but the ship could not settle still enough to set fast at the right spot, so the pilot and tug boats left. After sunup they returned again and we brought in chains and anchors dripping with mud that reeked of sewage. The next attempt to reset them succeeded.

Captain Marrón and Harry wanted to take me on shore leave in this city of nearly 150,000 where they knew some women. They had to be aboard during the beginning of unloading oil to the thermoelectric plant so we agreed to meet in town and I took a walk about first.

Cienfuegos—which means one hundred fires—is a lovely colonial style city known for its cleanliness, for its efficient bus system and rational distribution of farm products. I first strolled about the wide wharf. Looking at the many docked freighters, I came upon a small cargo ship I'd recognized from television, the Hermann. Despite having been patched up in Mexico, dents made by canon and machine-gun fire from a US coast guard speed boat were visible. It made me angry, thinking of how the nation of my birth behaves towards people who refuse to cow tow to its profiteering dictates. Staring at the Hermann gave me goose bumps too, remembering how 11 men, armed only with knives and machetes, defied the aggressors. A true David and Goliath story.

On the morning of January 25, 1990, the Hermann sailed out of Moa, Holguín, the principle nickel port. The 3,600-ton displacement freighter was carrying ten tons of chrome to Tampico where it would load 15 tons of merchandise. Like many ships throughout the world, the Hermann flew a Panamanian flag of convenience. The Hermann was officially owned by Guamar Shipping Company S.A., but chartered and operated exclusively by Cuba.

This is the story told by the Hermann crew with factual evidence to back much of it up.

Crossing the Yucatán Canal on January 29, a US reconnaissance aircraft repeatedly overflew the small ship. The next day, US coast guard cutter, WPB-1320 Chiconteague, began maneuvers around the 80-meter long freighter. US sailors shouted insults and made vulgar gestures to the

Cuban crew. The Yankee captain demanded that Captain Diego Sanchez Serrano heave to and allow his ship to be inspected for "possible drugs". Without hesitation, and without consulting Havana authorities, the captain and the entire crew told the Yankees to take a flying leap. The cutter shot high-pressured water at the crew. Angel Bertot Gutiérrez, the 60-year old cook and former guerrilla in the Rebel Army, dashed out of the kitchen onto the main deck with cleaver in hand. The coast guard threatened again to board but Captain Sanchez never wavered course.

The US State Department advised the Cuban government that it presumed the right to inspect the ship despite the fact that the Hermann was in international waters. Captain Sanchez contacted Cuban government leaders, who asked for his assessment of the situation and what the crew wanted to do. No one wanted to give in. The government leaders agreed and so informed Washington DC.

The Hermann stayed on course to Tampico.

The Chiconteague rammed the Hermann just before dawn on the last day of January but the Cuban freighter was able to outmaneuver the cutter's many attempts to fatally ram it. US sailors then opened fire, hitting the hull, decks, bridge, storehouse and machine department with canon balls and machine gun bullets. They fired repeatedly for one hour and forty-five minutes. Miraculously, no one was injured but the ship was damaged. Passing by Mexican oil rigs that could have been set on fire by US bullets, the Hermann managed to limp into Mexican waters and the cutter backed off.

Mexican officials in Tampico inspected the ship for any trace of drugs at the request of the Cuban government. Fidel later said: "They found neither drugs nor urine, neither drugs nor shit on that ship! I'm certain that if those dogs had been taken on the U.S. coast guard vessel, all three things would have been found there."

The day after the Hermann docked and after being inspected, the crew flew to Havana to attend an emotional rally held only a few score meters from the United States Interest Section. I stood with thousands more beside a huge billboard the government had long ago set before the aggressors building. It read: "Mister imperialists, we have absolutely no fear." Standing under the headless monument to the U.S. battleship Maine (1), Fidel presented the 11 heroes to a cheering crowd. He used descriptions and a style that nearly every Cuban could agree and identify with.

"They wanted to provoke and test the morale of Cubans, because every time they commit a crime they think others will be frightened. They fail to realize that such crimes increase the courage of our people..."

Fidel explained the events of engagement and what he told Cuba's representatives in Washington.

"If they tell you the ship has a Panamanian flag, you tell them that the flag is Panamanian but the balls on it are Cuban. The crew refused to be searched as a matter of honor and because it had no confidence in the shitty U.S. navy and authorities, because they are capable of making up any lie and of planting anything on the ship."

The men on the Hermann "waged a moral war against the enemy...When the ship could catch on fire, when they no longer had life preservers, when they had no chance of saving themselves unless they surrendered, they didn't stop, they continued on course and continued to be willing to run aground or crash into the oil rigs and burn to death there rather than fall into the hands of the imperialists...You have here these men, simple men of the people, turned into heroes overnight."

United Nations Council of States heard Cuba's formal protest the following week but took no action against the United States' unprovoked aggression in international waters. US representative, Thomas Pickering, arrogantly asserted his government's "right" to inspect the Hermann, and insisted that similar actions could occur in the future. As if to show the Yankees what Cuba's response would be, the Communist party elected Hermann helmsman Francisco Montalvo Peñalver to its central committee.

I met Harry and Marrón at the post office. The captain was known by his last name by many of us when off duty. Married with three daughters, he was devoted to his family and, like most Cuban men, loved to chase women on the side.

"Hey, Ron, just hold on a few minutes," Harry said. "I have to send a telegram to my wife. I always do so from each port."

"Ron, you got your weapons with you?" Marrón asked.

"Weapons? What do you mean?"

"You know, pen and notebook in back pocket."

I reached into my back pocket.

"Shit. I forgot to leave them."

"Well, just don't use them. Keep them hidden. We want to have a good time and not scare anyone. No politics, hey."

Harry came out of the post office as I nodded my head: "Right! Only fun."

"That's done. OK, you guys, let's stop by a friend's house to say hello. I'll ask Lucía where we might go out. There's so many places closed these days."

Harry directed us down a side street and stopped in front of a door divided in two horizontal parts. A sign glued to it read: "Se permuta a Habana." (2)

A loose-skinned, platinum blond came to the door. Her light brown eyes lit up when she saw Harry.

"I knew it. I knew you'd come. I was telling Margo that you'd be stopping by this very night. I saw it in the shells. Margo, look, it's Harry," she squealed, waving her flabby arms about.

Another white, fat woman waddled up and hugged big Harry. They all talked at once. Marrón and I were introduced. Lucía's son walked into the living room and touched Harry's head hair.

"What did you do with your hair, Harry?" the boy asked with an adult air.

"That's the way Africans comb their hair, Raúl."

"Yeah? Well, it looks terrible. You've gotten balder and fatter since the last time I saw you."

Harry laughed heartedly, his head tilted back.

"That's my boy. Always straight-forward, this one. Eight years old and already a little man."

A little smart-aleck, I thought.

Harry and the two women exchanged stories while the captain and I sat silently on the plastic covered sofa. Lucía got up and served us the last of her rum. Margo asked me if I was an officer. As I explained who I was, her gray-blue eyes widened and darkened.

"Look, don't worry about Ron," Harry interjected. "He's aplatanado (3)

"OK, Harry, whatever you say. Your friends are mine," Margo replied and patted my face. broadly.

The women went into the kitchen and we men huddled.

"I asked Lucía where we might go," Harry said. "She said it's difficult. Few places are open. You have to make reservations well in advance and there's almost no rum. It's gotten as bad as Havana. She wants us to stay. I think we might just as well go find some rum and party here."

Marrón and I looked at one another. He seemed pleased. I shrugged. They told me to keep the women company while they scrounged for rum. Lucía went to shower and Margo sat close beside me on the couch. She told me she worked in a state safety inspection office concerning industrial accidents. Her former husband was a merchant marine, just like Lucia's ex. A woman and child came up to the front door. The top half of the door was open and I could see a terrific body from the waist up. Her breasts spread across a broad chest, sticking straight out. Large pointed nipples pressed against a pretty black and white blouse. Her face was naturally smooth and opaque. She called out for Lucía in a deep voice. Lucía yelled from the bathroom for her to come in. The powerfully built woman swung open the door with a flick of one hand, revealing firm rounded hips, suggestively outlined in tight pants. She swayed gracefully past me without batting an eye my way. Wow!

"You like dark girls, Ron?" Margo asked coldly, her eyes sparking.

"I like what is attractive."

Harry and the captain returned with two bottles of Decano, a decent rum from Villa Clara, bottled in soft drink-sized bottles. A bartender had sold them through the back door for 20 pesos each. Legally, Decano sold for seven.

Lucía bounced into the small living room dressed in a low-cut blouse and white shorts. She was all painted up. Lucía introduced us to her luscious friend, Angel. Her daughter went to play with Raúl and she sat down for a drink. Lucía put down a bucket of ice, a handful of Tropicola soft drinks and a couple limes. I made Cuba Libres while she put music on her tape recorder. I stole glances at Angel, who sat quietly with her hands folded, while Margo kept jabbering in my ear. Margo wanted to dance, so we moved about the floor: she thrusting her bumpy stomach and lumpy tits into my body. Marrón was getting chummy with Lucía and Harry sat politely with Angel.

We were running out of rum and Margo was irritating me. I wanted Angel. The more I showed a lack of interest in her, the more Margo tugged at me. I asked Harry to come with me to hunt down more rum. We walked up and down many streets. Bars and restaurants were closed. We stopped a man who told us to go to Tomas' a couple blocks away. He was fresh out but told us to try Mamuñas place. "She usually has some. If not, then there ain't none in town."

Although it was midnight, there were still people hanging out on stoops. Some were conducting neighborhood guard duty, a nightly task of each block committee (4). We came around a corner and faced a large, paint-pealed, wooden house still lit up with its doors open and people cleaning up inside. We asked a boy where Mamuña was. An elderly, fat woman emerged.

"You fellas sailors?"

"Yep," replied Harry, flashing her his divine dandy smile.

"What ship you on?" the bushy-haired dark woman asked in a raspy voice.

"Seaweed."

"Ah, I know that one—the big tanker. Well, I guess you want some rum?"

"What have you got?"

"The usual. Ronda."

"Forty do for two bottles?" Harry asked.

"Sure enough."

Mamuña went inside and I caught a glimpse of someone in the kitchen throwing a bucket of water over the floor. A trickle of blood streamed out onto the dirt. A couple of dressed up dolls sat rumpled in a corner. Harry speculated that a toque de santo (5) had been conducted, complete with a sacrificed animal. Harry thought Mamuña was the medium.

When we got back to the house, the captain and Lucía were dancing gaily. Margo sat alone looking bored. Angel was dozing in an armchair. Harry stirred Angel with an open bottle of rum held under her nose. I poured shots for Margo and me and danced with her. When the number ended I asked Angel to dance. She held me close; we didn't stop dancing when the number ended. I kissed her ear and ran my tongue up her long thick neck. She offered her pliant lips and didn't wait for me to take them. She kissed, she danced, she looked just like her name. Angel didn't speak. She just kept rubbing her body over mine. My penis got so stiff it hurt, cramped as it was behind a zipper. She said she had to be at work at 7:00 a.m. and had to go home with her daughter. She lived with her parents and her brother's family. It was already 2:00 a.m. and we had nowhere to go. She led us away from Margo's stares into the kitchen. Angel pressed my face between her strong palms and sucked my lips. Tickling my ears with her agile fingers, she ground her cunt into my cock. I rubbed her churning rump with one hand while tracing my other fingers over the front of her pants. Her hard nipples pressed into my chest, now shirtless.

"Rub my tits; rub them hard," she demanded huskily.

I kneaded her compact globes and kissed her lips hard, bitingly. Her tongue filled my mouth. She rimmed my ear with her serpent tongue. I couldn't hold back nor was it Angel's intention that I should. When there's no place to go and you're horny that's what Cuban dancing is all about—and the juice shot over my underwear.

It was three in the morning as I walked Angel and her daughter home. I could hardly restrain myself I was so horny for this woman. She said she'd be here for me when I returned with more oil for her town.

Back at Lucía's, Margo was waiting for me with a vengeance.

"Tu, con una negra! Como puedes preferir una negra por me?" (6)

"You show contempt for Margo," Lucía sided with Margo.

I was surprised by this racist attitude, not what I usually encountered in Cuba. I felt like I was in southern United States. I wanted to tell them it was easy to choose Angel over puffy flesh and petulance, but I held my tongue.

"You degrade me, you shit!" Margo screamed and dug her long painted nails into my underarm. She pulled me into the kitchen, her nails intact. I could understand that she felt rejected and angry but I couldn't quarter her bitterness turned into racial prejudice. I was lost for words and she seized upon my silence as an opening to impress me with her lingering desire mixed with jealous anger. She relaxed her fingernail grip and jammed me into a wall with her body. She squirmed over me and tried to kiss me. I fended her off.

"Margo, I'm sorry," I spoke softly. "I don't want to hurt you but I don't care for racial prejudice nor do I want to have sex with you."

She stopped gyrating and looked at me coldly. I walked into the living room to find the captain with Lucía and Harry sitting quietly with drinks in their hands. Dawn would be coming soon and it was time to return to ship. Harry and I left the captain and said we'd see him at the launch.

On the way back, Harry and I mused about the evening.

"I've known those women a long time, Ron, and I never heard such prejudice from them before. They both have had black lovers."

"It's one thing for them to choose their bed partners but when it comes down to it they think they are better than black folks," I said. "Margo was indignant not only because her advances fell flat but that her white skin didn't impress me more than a black woman's. She must realize that Angel is more attractive, sexier, than she, but she thinks she's `purer' simply because she's white. This is a typical attitude in the United States, but I hadn't encountered it before in Cuba."

"No. Racism is not allowed in any official or public way since the Revolution. But there are still a lot of white people with superiority complexes left over," Harry said.

We reached the dock and Harry showed his seaman's credentials to a customs guard and walked through the gate. I showed the official my letter of permission to sail. The guard studied it.

"Where is the original?" he asked, dryly.

"The captain has it on the ship where it should be," I said, irritatedly.

"This is a copy. You can't pass with this. I have to see the original."

"You must be kidding," I replied, baffled.

"No. I am not. You can't pass," he said, evenly.

I looked at Harry and he shook his head, the perennial smile gone.

"Look. This is crazy. I've been on this ship for weeks and have stopped at other ports without this problem. I was explicitly told by the port authority major in Havana that the original letter must be given to the captain of the ship. He signed and stamped it, as did the director of the shipping company and a security officer."

The guard wasn't listening. Dead panned, he blocked the gateway with his stiff body.

I heard a customs woman inside the guard's office exclaim: "Imagine! Here is a white foreigner with this moreno, and both of them drunk."

Harry jerked his head in her direction.

"What did you say? Why does it have to be a moreno? I'm the chief engineer of one of Cuba's largest tankers. I am a seaman and a member of the Communist party. What the hell does the color of my skin have to do with anything?"

The official on duty emerged from inside the office shack. He was as black as Harry. He gazed at Harry but said nothing. He took my letter from the guard and began reading it.

I couldn't contain myself.

"Harry, imagine this scene. Three guards with nothing to do. It's obvious they are bored and want a bit of entertainment to keep them awake. Bureaucrats! Just what Fidel talks about. They feel smart holding up our ship, which is ready to sail, in order to load another 16,000 tons of fuel for their electricity. What does that matter to bored bureaucrats!"

That was not the right thing to say.

The head guard stared meanly at me.

"Get out of here. You wait across the street until the chief of security comes on duty," he ordered.

"When might that be?" I asked, flippantly.

"Eight o'clock."

"That's two hours from now. Our ship is supposed to sail at 07:00."

"That is no concern of mine. You lack respect. And you," he said, pointing at Harry, "you wait with him."

"That will delay the ship," Harry said, quietly.

The officer had spoken. He walked into his shack.

Harry and I walked across the street.

"We'll have to wait for the captain. He'll resolve this," Harry said, and clamed up.

We waited in silence until the captain came wavering down the street as the sun rose. He had a tipsy grin on his face and greeted us with hands waving. His gayety disappeared as Harry explained the situation.

"All right, you stay here. I'll resolve this," he stated irritatedly, already sobering up.

The captain crossed the street and flashed his credentials at the surly guard and walked into the shack. A few minutes later he crossed the street and told us the officer wouldn't budge.

"You must wait for the chief. The man is still angry at your 'lack of respect,' Ron."

Captain Marrón said he'd arrange for a launch to take us to ship after this got cleared up. He still hadn't found a ride when the chief of security drove up to the gate. He conferred with the officer on duty and then the captain. Captain Marrón motioned for us to come through the gate. The chief of security handed me my letter and filled out an "incident report". We were now free to find our way to the ship. Three small craft pilots turned us down: "No fuel". A tug boat pilot told the captain he'd just taken the harbor pilot to our ship. He reluctantly agreed to take us.

It was 09:00 by the time we climbed up the rope ladder; the gangway had already been lifted. The main deck was filled with grinning crewmen as we swung aboard.

"Ignore them, Ron," Harry breathed through clenched teeth. He climbed down the stairwell to the engine room and I followed behind the captain up the bridge where the pilot was pacing. The mooring lines were ordered in. Two hours late, we were sailing back to Santiago de Cuba to reload for another trip to Cienfuegos.

Well out to sea, Sigi, Harry, the captain and I drank coffee in his disorderly cabin. The captain recounted the incident at the customs gate to Sigi, referring to the guards as "comemierdas" (7).

"No problem. When we return to Cienfuegos, you'll be restricted to ship. No shore leave for you, Ron," the first mate told me with a straight face.

I was aghast.

"You see, Ron, besides the 'lack of respect' matter," Captain Marrón lectured, "you gotta be less choosy and more sensitive to the moment. You gotta take the woman offered. It's not comradely to put a monkey wrench in the arrangements."

"But that's not democratic!" I protested. "I wasn't consulted nor was Angel."

"There he goes again," said the first mate. "A social evening out is not a subject for democracy. You take what you can get, what is offered, and respect the ambiance. You get the pretty one next time, perhaps. That is the seaman's way."

Brown bubbles sprouted up. They percolated. Growing bigger and bigger. Coming nearer and nearer. I attacked them with my pick and burst some but they multiplied faster than I could bust them. I grabbed an electric pick hammer and shattered one after another. The bubbles burst into crackling pieces that flew into my cheeks and eyes.

I tossed awake. I was lying on wet sheets. My body bathed in sweat. My nightmare reflected a day scrapping rust on the main deck near the tanks. We had been loading crude oil at the refinery and deckhands were removing rust. Some of the rust close to the tank tops was too thick to remove with hand picks so the electric tool was used against the safety rules. Electric instruments are prohibited while loading and unloading. A spark could set off an explosion or fire or both. A refinery guard stood on the quay watching us work. It made me nervous but the men said that crude petroleum is not "too dangerous". They said they wouldn't use the electric pick around white gas products but crude is OK. I wasn't convinced.

On route to Cienfuegos, I spent the day scraping rust. After dinner, Captain Marrón called me to the bridge. Sigi and the radio officer stood beside him. They all looked grim. The captain spoke in a serious tone.

"Look at this radio message we just received, Ron."

"Captain Marrón of the Seaweed you are hereby instructed that the North American citizen, Ron Ridenour, is not to leave ship. Place him in a separate cabin and keep him from the crew until further instructed." Col. Rúben Quintana/MININT

"This must be a prank," I said, perplexed.

"What did you do in Santiago de Cuba before we met at the night club, Ron?" Captain Marrón asked sternly without responding to my comment.

"Nothing. After Nautico, I got too drunk to remember. Tómas took me home. You know that."

"Well, you must have done something serious at some point. Or maybe it's related to the incident in Cienfuegos. This could put your future in Cuba in jeopardy. You could create problems for me too. I can't afford to have you going around causing trouble when you're under my responsibility. We'll have to do as instructed. From her on you eat in the officer's mess and keep away from the men. Keep to your cabin or to the first's."

I was flabbergasted.

Sigi recalled a time when the Ministry of Interior (MININT) instructed the captain of a ship he sailed on to place the chief engineer and chief petty officer under cabin arrest with armed guard.

"But I trust Ron. He's a good worker and a friend. We won't put him under guard. And Ron," he looked at me solemnly, "I'll testify for you."

"This must be a grave matter whatever it is," the radio officer put in, "because MININT sent the message in code exclusively over our radio. No other ship can make it out."

"Yeah, Ron knows about codes. Far more than we do. Don't you, Ron?" Captain Marrón said sarcastically. He was either referring to the book I wrote about the CIA and Cuba, or inferring that I was more intimately connected to the CIA than met the eye.

I didn't like the sinister tone. They couldn't be for real my brain, my heart told me, but they showed no sign of doubt. I had to go along and see where it took me. I spent the next hours reading in my cabin. I ate with the officers and returned to my "cell". Sigi knocked on my door and told me I could take a stretch on the bridge. The captain, radio officer and a helmsman were there. They all nodded to me but were tight-lipped. We were a few hours out of Cienfuegos when the VHF radio phone rang. The captain picked up the receiver. A voice could be heard saying to switch to channel 8, a channel I had not heard used before. The voice returned:

"Regarding North American citizen Ron Ridenour you have aboard: keep him apart from the crew until docked in Cienfuegos where he'll be interrogated by Captain Reyes. Over."

"Roger. Who is this? Over."

"Captain Fernando López of Cienfuegos port authorities. Over."

"Roger. Over and out."

The captain replaced the phone and looked at me curiously.

"You are a disciplined man, Ron," the captain said, in a man-to-man tone. "Stay in your cabin until Cienfuegos. We'll have breakfast brought to you."

"What about all the rust and the men? If I don't show my face they'll wonder what's going on."

"Don't worry about the rust, Ron. There will always be rust and sailors to scrape it. The men, well, they'll think you're doing intellectual work in your cabin, that's all."

I was perplexed about all this and a bit worried now. I bedded down early. Next morning, a steward brought me coffee and bread. I then went to Sigi's cabin to wash. He wasn't his usual jolly self. In the early afternoon, we entered Cienfuegos harbor. I was allowed on bridge. The captain received another call over VHF concerning "La paloma" (8). He replied: "The pigeon is under control and will not fly."

Sigi looked at me sorrowfully.

"No matter what happens we'll always be brothers," he said forlornly.

I felt maudlin. I went to my cabin and dressed in my clean, pressed uniform, preparing for the "interrogation". Back on the bridge, the political officer showed me a letter of recommendation for me which he, the captain, the union steward and the party secretary had all signed.

"Harry and I will go to the port authorities and find out what this is all about, Ron, and let you know when we return," the captain said. He and Harry, dressed smartly, walked out of the bridge.

"Hey, wait a minute. I'll come with you."

"No. You know what the instructions are. You must stay in your cabin or with Sigi," the captain asserted authoritatively.

I didn't know what to think. I was downcast. I had ached to be with Angel and now this. The captain and Harry didn't return until the next morning. They laughed when they saw my sad face. "Angel is waiting for you, Ron," Harry said, grinning from ear to ear. "We assured her you'd be there tonight. There were problems with your papers, you know."

"You are now free to come and go as before," Captain Marrón said, chortling. "We worked it out with the port authorities. You needn't worry any longer."

"Well, that's a relief. What was it all about? Was this some sort of joke or was I under suspicion because of the gate 'incident'?"

They laughed.

"Ron, you're famous at the port authorities and customs."

That's all they'd tell me. I took the next launch to town and found Angel and a hotel.

Notes:

1. Upon overthrowing Batista, jubilant demonstrators beheaded the monument of its eagle. The Maine had exploded in Havana's harbor, February 15, 1898, causing the death of 241 crewmen. The United States government cast blame on the Spanish, whose troops were being defeated by the Cuban mambisas. Newspaper magnate William Randolph Hearst spread a propaganda campaign against the Spanish and demanded that the US go to war. Two months later, the U.S. government declared war against Spain just in time to prevent the Cuban liberation army from achieving full victory and thus independence. The U.S. government with its mightier army was able to force the first Cuban government to accept many anti-sovereign concessions, such as the eternal leasing of much land and a bay in Guantánamo province where the US built its Guantánamo naval base, infamous today for where the US tortures Arabic people.

At the rally, Fidel blasted the aggressor Yankees with all the vigor the big man could muster.

"I wouldn't say that the sailors who died on the Maine didn't deserve a monument...because they were the victims of an imperialist crime. Historical research and all indications show how convenient and odd it was that all the officers were taken ashore to a party. The humble sailors on that battleship, at a time when the empire was about to wage its first imperialist war, were mercilessly sacrificed. There's every clue that the imperialists themselves blew up the ship...That was the pretext used for war, the pretext for intervention in Cuba, the occupation of the Philippines, Puerto Rico and other Spanish possessions. It was like the well-known prefabricated Gulf of Tonkin incident, which took place (against Vietnam) in more recent years."

"If there's one thing we can be certain of, it is that never again will the voracious eagle which symbolizes the empire be restored on top of these columns..."

The Maine's captain told his government that the explosion was not set but caused by accident.

2. Seeking to exchange flat for one in Havana.
3. A transplanted foreigner, as regular a Cuban as anybody.
4. Comites de Defense Revolucionaria (CDR)-Revolutionary Defense Committees.
5. Ritual for a saint.
6. "You, with a negro woman. How could you prefer a negra for me?"
7. Shit-eaters.
8. The pigeon.

CHAPTER FOUR: SEAWEED RETIRES

After an ecstatic night with tigress Angel, I soaked my tingling pores floating in the hotel pool. Angel had left to breakfast with her daughter. At midday, I climbed aboard the Seaweed and we set out on the last leg of my bojeo—482 nautical miles to Havana. We would first unload the rest of our petroleum at Mariel, close to the capital.

Sitting bareback at the stem of the bow, the mid-morning sun caressed my body as I read, "The Mambo Kings Play Songs of Love," a jazzy novel by Oscar Hijuelos, a native-born Cuban raised in New York City. My blood flowed with the speed of the ship cutting through the downy serene sea, the engines purring beneath me. As I glanced up from the rhythm kings, I spotted land in the distance. We were passing Playa Girón, site of the April 1961 Bay of Pigs invasion, in which the CIA directed 1,300 Cuban paramilitary exiles from Miami. Within 72 hours, 120 invaders had been killed and the remaining forces were captured by Cuban militia in Matanzas province and army troops. This was the first military defeat for U.S. imperialism. Among the 1,197 captured paramilitarists, 100 had been plantation owners, 35 had been industrial magnates, 200 others had been big businessmen and property owners, 194 were ex-soldiers of Batista, including 14 wanted for murder and torture during the revolutionary war. Their leaders were ransomed for one million dollars and the remainder were eventually returned to the US for an additional $62 million.

After leaving the huge Zapata Swamp area, we headed west toward the Isle of Youth, formerly the Isle of Pioneers. Robert Lewis Stevensen's, "Treasure Island", made the island world famous. Instead of pirates, the island now houses thousands of foreign students from Third World lands, and poor students from the United States, who study medicine free of charge. The only condition the Cuban government makes is that upon graduation they return to their native land to treat the sick.

The wind was still; the sky was blue spotted with fluffy cirrus cumulus clouds. The hills of Siquanea and Cañada peered at me above citrus orchards. In those hills lay Cuba's largest and one of the world's richest deposits of marble, a significant source of the island's economy. Frothy ocean and land dissolve into reefs and shoals, fusing into one fascination. Beaches glisten with brilliant multi-colored stones and white sand.

From the Isle of Youth, we continued west and were soon circling the westernmost cape, Cabo San Antonio. In a few hours, we were zig zagging through a narrow, treacherous channel into Mariel harbor—site of the 1980 exodus of about 120,000 dissatisfied Cubans beguiled by President Jimmy Carter's "open arms policy", welcoming a "better economic life of freedom" in the United States. Locals in Mariel call their town Fort Chaffey after the location where these Cubans fled

We docked in front of the busy thermoelectric plant, which also serves part of Havana. Another ship was unloading at the neighboring cement factory. A few of its crew hopped over to chat with friends on the Seaweed. It turned into a family reunion complete with a bottle of uncut sugar cane alcohol, colao.

Captain Marrón greeted our visitors, two of whom had sailed with him on another ship. Their conversation did not include port life with women. The next day, Leon and Benito mentioned the "queens aboard ship last night" as "great guys and good sailors". I was surprised as I had not noticed their sexual identities.

"They are queers and our friends," the boatswain told me, matter-of-factly. "There aren't many homosexuals in the maritime industry but there is no discrimination or abuse towards the few there are, not like before the revolution and in its early years."

In the heat of the afternoon, I dove 15 meters from the bow's stem into the relatively clean bay. In my skin-diving gear, I swam across the bay to a foundered fishing boat where I found many varieties of fish: parrot, pig, jack, small red fish akin to red snappers, and one long and glaring barracuda. It took me two hours before finally spearing two flat silver jacks with my air compressor gun. The swim back to ship was choppy and tiring but I managed to bring the fish aboard and stored them in a galley freezer.

Some of the crew fished alongside locals off the quay where we were anchored. At sunset, some men returned with several small snappers they had hooked using snail bait. A party was soon underway with son music and bits of fried fish. Carmen, a steward, was the only woman dancing and she alternated partners until midnight, no worse the wear.

I awoke to find the bay stinking and blackened with crude oil. My heart sank. There'd be no fishing for some time now. I went to find the captain. He was in his quarters with the chief engineer and the first mate discussing the calamity, ascertaining what had happened and what to say to police inspectors expected anytime.

The oiler on the midnight shift had let loose the oil bilge after the donkeyman finished unloading the tanks. He admitted his deed. "I had no choice because the ship would have tilted if I sent the bilge to the designated tank. There was too much and it would have tipped the balance," he claimed.

The oiler, and the responsible machinist, tried to cover their asses by saying the bilge tank for residue oil was full. Harry said that it was not. Regardless, anyone could easily have watched for any tilting. If it occurred, it could be corrected by turning the proper valves to even out the weight. Anyway, as the chief engineer said, we were docked butted against the quay and nothing would have happened. So why did the oiler let the bilge loose and why had the machinist gone along? Lack of concern for their environment, for their mother sea, laziness. As Harry pointed out, it is certainly easier to pull one valve and let the oil out than be on the lookout for this and that.

Many seamen, just like most other humans, don't care enough. The only thing that seems to be potentially effective to stop polluting is to make it expensive for the polluter, including the ship-owner. And that was the next topic.

Captain Marrón was worried that the ship would be fined, in addition to the men responsible. It could have amounted to as much as 2000 pesos. Then the paperwork involved, and the "uptight company administration," made him most unhappy. In the end, he would look bad. Sigi didn't like it either because it would be his task to fill out all the papers.

I asked what the oiler and machinist could have been thinking. "Didn't they know their deed would be visible the next day?"

"That's just the problem with the Cuban culture. Most don't think of the consequences of their deeds. They only think of the moment, of resolving their problem for the moment," Captain Marrón replied, his jowls tight.

A life guided by what is convenient and pleasurable is inadequate to create socialism, I thought.

When the police came, they chatted amiably with the captain and the first mate. Captain Marrón apologized for what had happened, and added that there was nothing that could have been done. "There was a leak in one of the hose couplings. We're fixing it now."

Sure enough, men were hoisting up a hose onto the upper deck and tinkering with a coupling, which, in fact, did have a slight leak. Nevertheless, the "white lie" did not explain the main cause for the tons of crude in the bay. The police did not want any paperwork hassles either. Friendly relations with transporters of energy was more desirable. They let the incident slip.

It didn't feel good leaving Mariel bay an oil spill disaster, watching people sitting on the small sandy beach behind the fishing pier where no one was fishing. The only positive feeling I had was one of acceptance as a human being, a fellow colleague. No one, not even myself, had thought it was too delicate for me to be in on the conversation, which involved cheating the law. Furthermore, no one thought it necessary to caution me about saying anything to the police. While I felt warmed by their confidence, I also felt semi-guilty as an accomplice after the fact.

Two hours later, we reached Havana harbor. Port authorities told us to await docking instructions. Arturo was on watch.

"Port authorities must have known there was no free dock. They could have told us to come in later without all this waiting," he said, frustrated. "It's just the typical arbitrary attitude, lack of coordination. There is simply no concern for others having to needlessly wait. Waiting is just normal life. No one gets more or less money, food, health care, education, social security—or so they think. But dammit, it's my life that is being wasted. That's important to me."

Figure 7: Sailing past Havana harbor and fort.

This circumstance and Arturo's anger reminded me of something that took place during my short voyage with the Gold Sand, a trip I took while waiting between navigations on the Seaweed. Like the Seaweed, Gold Sand was one of Cuba's three large Soviet tankers. I sailed with her just one and one-half days from Puerto Padre, on the east coast, to Havana. Captain Aranguern had maintained the illusion the entire time we waited outside Havana that we'd get our berth "any hour now; don't worry". It took us 36 hours to get a berth, longer than the voyage.

On route with Gold Star, an elder deckhand spoke more frankly about The Waiting.

"A Cuban seaman must have patience above all else. We never depart or arrive on time. Coordination, timing are concepts foreign to our mentality and to our social system. We are always waiting," he said with great agitation, as he plied the line on his make-shift reel, hoping with all patience that he would catch a big fish.

Arturo lacked this man's patience. As we watched a ship sail out from the refinery, he said:

"I wonder how many ships are in front of us waiting to take her place?"

The departing ship complained to port authorities that we were too close to her. We were ordered out four miles to "Await further instructions".

Arturo and I passed much of the evening watch discussing job politics.

"Officers get better ships and quicker promotions," Arturo complained, "if they are socios (1) with administrators. A well-placed gift from a foreign port doesn't hurt either. If an honest man keeps his nose clean, keeps his ship in good shape, that is not enough. It's who you know that counts."

"That's pretty much the way it is the world over, I believe."

"That's no damn excuse for a socialist revolution, with our idealistic values of uplifting mankind. We should not fall into that same grime."

It was dark again when we finally got instructions that a berth awaited us. The lamps along malecón were lit as we sailed into port. The curving seawall sparkled lovingly. I realized why Havana harbor is known as the collar de perla (2), and I felt privileged and safe watching it, knowing that when I disembarked I need not fear being mugged or murdered on the way home. No crazed assassin or serial-killer awaited me.

Completing my goal, making the bojeo, it seemed only fitting that I should throw the first jibalay. Whirling the thin rope, I cast it far onto the wharf. It landed over the dock worker's head and he didn't scramble fast enough to catch it before it fell into the black liquid. I pulled it in and sailed it through the air again. This time he grabbed it and drew in the spring mooring line attached. He hung the loop around a bollard and the ship began to come to. Two long mooring lines were cast in the same manner. The spring line around a bitt on the bow had not been secured properly and it stretched too tautly. No other mooring line was as yet secured and the ship's movement weighed on the one spring line. It began to slip and burn. If it snapped, our heads would be in danger. Raymondo managed to throw another loop around the bitt, and it held the ship until the long lines tightened.

Relieved, I gazed over the starboard bow down at the wharf. Dutch seamen on the Shell tanker M/T Cauricas had painted in large white letters: "Amigos Indonesia-Holland. Muchos besos para senoritas cubanas". (3)

My voyage had ended. I didn't know it then but it was also the last long voyage for Seaweed. She would soon be put out to pasture.

Notes:

1. Friendly associates.
2. Pearl Necklace.
3. "Indonesian-Dutch friends. Many kisses for the Cuban women."

CHAPTER FIVE: SHARK

Figure 8: Captain Antonio Garcia Urquiolla. He had been a double agent within the CIA for Cuba's defense, and figures in Ridenour's book, "Backfire: The CIA's Biggest Burn".

My first sailing mission intent was not with the Seaweed. I came to the Seaweed because the first tanker I sought to sail with, the Shark, was crippled and under repairs between periodic short-distance exercises during the six weeks I was aboard. The Shark was my first objective because its captain, Antonio García Urquiola, had infiltrated the CIA as a double agent for the Cuban government. He had formed part of my book, "Backfire". The empire's covert warriors thought it had recruited the Shark's captain in 1978. They thought they had bought his aid in their efforts to sabotage his country's maritime economy, even his assistance in assassinating Fidel. Unbeknownst to the pernicious CIA, Urquiola was already "Aurelio," an agent for Cuba's state security (1).

Bright and early on the 4th of July 1990, 214 years after the newly formed United States Congress announced the Declaration of Independence from Great Britain's colonial power, I swung up a gangway onto the Shark. I was exhilarated, launching into this adventure, the very first citizen of the United States to have been accepted by the Cuban government to board a Cuban vessel and the first foreigner seeking to make the bojeo. It was a most appropriate day to celebrate, defying the nation of my birth, whose neo-colonial empire had placed the country of my choice under its canon.

Guillermo, the second mate, greeted me. He took me to the berth where I would be staying. I put down my gear and opened a port hole. Then Guillermo took me on a tour of the ship that would be my home for the coming weeks, most of it anchored at Havana's harbor. I would periodically return to my apartment since the Shark seldom sailed out more than a few sea miles.

The Shark was one of five Rumanian ships that Cuba bought in 1987. They were of the same build: 102 meters long and 16 meters wide, and carried 4,000 tons of petroleum. The crew referred to these tankers as "Rumalas", roughly translated to mean "bad Rumanian", because they are the result of shoddy work designed for the "socialist camp". Unlike on other tankers, the tanks were on deck and oil was always slopping out making the deck slippery and dangerous. There were many other complaints: the berths were extremely small; the laundry machine was always breaking down; the air conditioning only worked sporadically; the DDR-built engine valves frequently stuck, which was the current cause of this breakdown.

Crew members often smoked and watched TV in the officers' lounge where we gathered after lunch. "Here, it don't matter who you are. You can use either lounge as long as you come in clean," explained Zenia, the chubby chambermaid.

After coffee, Guillermo took me to the captain's cabin, a spacious spick-and-span, two-room "apartment" complete with kitchen and bathroom. The captain sat at his desk bent over paperwork; a photo of Fidel hung on the wall behind him. When he looked up, he smiled thinly and extended a long arm to shake hands. His squinting eyes and hesitant manner indicated curious skepticism about my presence. We had only met once nearly three years before when I had interviewed him.

The pilot arrived as we stood searching for words. The relieved captain invited me on the bridge to observe the test maneuver. All equipment is checked during test maneuvers. The radio and telegraph bip behind the wheelhouse. Water valves, hoses and fire extinguishers are inspected. The sticky engine valves were to be retested.

On the bridge, the pilot leaned over the starboard bulwark and called to the helmsman, "Dead Slow." Rafael raised the engine telegraph forward one notch from "Stop," which sent a mechanical signal to the engine room to engage the engine. When the dial logged in at "Dead Slow", Rafael called out: "Dead Slow."

The slim helmsman wore dark sunglasses over mustachioed thin lips. Rafael was known as "the "teacher", because he had taught English in high school and later to naval officers. He changed careers to get away from the "boring routine of teaching and to earn more money". As a helmsman he earned double what teachers do.

After casting off, I climbed down into the engine room. It was so noisy I couldn't hear the men speak. A thermometer registered 45 degrees. Only the central control station was air conditioned. The engineer and an oiler were awaiting instructions from the bridge to move the telegraph to the speed ordered. All velocities were tested during the maneuver we made by the coastline. When we were several miles out, the pilot ordered "heave to", and the ship slowly came to a halt.

I rushed up to the bridge to find the captain three sheets under the wind, "cussing like a sailor".

"Those fucking `Mechanics'! What the fuck good are they? They are trained in Rumania, that's where. Incapable, that's what their socialism is!"

The chief engineer explained that the maneuver showed that the engine was still not functioning properly. A main valve kept sticking, causing the engine to start and stop, "when it fucking well pleases".

"Turn this fucking tub around and dock the bastard," the captain boomed. Rafael signaled the telegraph and shifted direction. He and the others on the bridge did not show disrespect for the captain but it seemed that they did not wish to hear his diatribe.

The chief engineer spoke again.

"No one is sicker of it than I am. We've had the valve out time and again, and now it has to be pulled out again. But I'm not going to touch the prick. The company is going to have to send real mechanics who know this engine. They'll have to get parts from somewhere. There are none here."

"Imagine!" the captain responded. "We had the fucker checked out in Romania just last month. It is only three years old and fucked already. Romanians were not real socialists! They never were."

On July 6, 1987, Cuban television screened the first episode of an 11-part video series entitled, "The CIA War Against Cuba". The first evening set the stage for the upcoming programs that would uncloak 27 double agents for Cuba's national security. Captain Antonio García Urquiola was the first. Their testimony about CIA officials, operating clandestinely under diplomatic cover inside Cuba, revealed how the Company initiated scores, perhaps hundreds, of assassination plots against President Fidel Castro, how it infected crops, animals and human beings with bacteriological warfare, subverted, or sought to, the nation's foreign trade, and disseminated disinformation about Cuba—all crimes by international law.

The graceful, olive-skinned captain invited me to his berth after our first test maneuver together. He was feeling morbid and wanted to drink and talk. He drank Cuba's best rum—in my opinion—Matusalém. Distilled for seven years, the brown cane is as smooth as cognac. Urquiola also drank Czechoslovakia's finest beer, Urquell. Both are hard to get in Cuba but the captain had a large private stock, which he offered to share with me. He had much on his chest.

"I've been a merchant marine since 1960 when I was 19 years old, and a captain since I was 28 years old. I captioned cargo ships for Mambisa, sailing to many foreign ports. On one such voyage in Amsterdam, `Norman' offered me $360 a month to become a CIA mole inside Cuba. The CIA offer was one I did not wish to refuse; I'd been waiting a dozen years for this ever since I associated with our Department of State Security. Norman gave me the code name `Alejandro'. I was already `Aurelio' for DSE.

"The Agency asked me to renounce my active captaincy to become an inspector, in order that I could be ashore more and thus gather the information they wanted. It hurt me to give up my ship. I loved the San Martí and my life at sea. It pained me as well to lead a triple life: the real me, another person for the CIA, and yet another for our intelligence agency. I lost my membership in the Communist party because intelligence was preparing me. I had to fake an attitude of apathy toward politics. My comrades and colleagues criticized me. I would sometimes think it necessary to say things that were not really me. My wife became estranged from me. She thought I was carousing with women when I was actually conducting my double agent duties. I felt very lonely."

Slowly he straightened his lank body. He stepped cat-like to the refrigerator where he drew out two more Urquells.

"The decision to come above ground had long been in the works. There were many reasons. I was suddenly ordered to Havana from Nuevitas port without explanation; something big was in the wind and I felt under great psychological pressure. Had I done something wrong? A few days later, the announcement came. Our security people visited my home and told my wife and daughter what to expect when they watched television that night. I was filmed making a mark on a bench in Havana, a signal for a rendezvous with a CIA official concerning a plot to assassinate Fidel. But this initial scene was shown in a vague way, such that it could lead to confusion about my real role. They told me not to report to work the next day. Sure enough, many comrades thought the program implied I was with the CIA. The second night my case came out fully. From that day forward my life changed completely. My daughter had been sad and upset with me, thinking I had turned pro-US. She was euphoric after viewing the television programs. The house filled with people celebrating. I was almost as surprised as they were when we watched the documentaries. I had little idea of the extensive documentation that our people had concerning CIA subversion.

"Yeah, everybody was happy. But another new stage, and a most difficult one, had begun. I had to readapt to reality, overcome those other persons I'd internalized. Even though they weren't me, they were there. Sometimes I wanted to touch my other selves, and they seemed to want to appear. They are especially present when I feel impotent. It was weird. It still is, like now when I can't resolve anything with the Shark. Those other me inside rebel.

"After the denunciation, Seguridad (2) told me to relax, take a vacation, enjoy myself. But it was too difficult for me. It took those two persons inside me many years to develop their personalities and it will come to take more years for them to go away.

"I had to work, to get back to normal. That was difficult too. DSE wouldn't let me travel out of the country—for my safety—yet that was my specialty: directing a ship, sailing cargo far and wide. Instead, I was offered an office job. I can't stand offices. I knew `Gallego' Meléndez over at Caribe. Unbeknownst to me, of course, he had also been a double agent. He got me a ship, one that only sails oil products around the island. This was new to me and brought more hardships. Everybody knew me to be a former security double agent.

"After 15 days training, they gave me the captainship of the old 7th of November. Although I had never sailed a tanker before, I had no problems with her. But it hit me all the harder sailing the cabotaje. I was enclosed, unable to sail abroad. I'd lost something important to my life. I hadn't been stable before but my life hadn't been monotonous as it is now. I even feel impotent. I lost this pride sailors have of creating their own world on their own ship. When I have a ship over a long period, I establish classes for officers: instruct in the navigational use of stars, weather conditions, international maritime law, ecological care, when and how to abandon ship, how to survive in the ocean. We also gave classes to crew members who wanted to become helmsmen, and we taught some English and maritime laws. We instructed how to defend the ship within the national strategy of `War of all the people' (3). I haven't done that in years because I kept getting shifted from ship to ship, because they either break down or they must sail abroad without me. After three years of this, I was given the Shark with the assurance that it will be mine for a good period. And what happens? The damn thing breaks down and nobody knows what to do about it. Ay caramba! (4)

"I want my own ship, dammit! One that works and one that I can sail on abroad. I want to create my own world again. The life of a merchant marines on a dry cargo ship is more tranquil. One has more time to sail, to reflect, to give courses, to get to know the men aboard and people ashore. On these cabotajes our lives are more agitated, constantly coming and going.

"The security people fucked me! Being a double agent fucked me! Carajo! (5)

"The CIA won't do anything to me now, I don't think. Maybe before. Maybe if they'd discovered who I was when I was still with them. But now they would have nothing to gain. They are intelligent too; they don't commit violence stupidly. They knew the risks they took recruiting me, recruiting all of us. They thought that money could buy us, even if we were true patriots, even Cuban security agents. They thought that once we had made contact with capitalism we'd become convinced of their 'superior way of life', and come over for real. They were dead WRONG!"

Figure 9: Throwing line to anchor, "Shark", 1990.

I went to work on the lower bridge while we all waited for the repairs. I squatted or sat on the hard deck scraping rust with a pick hammer, then sanded with an electric tool. I wore plastic goggles. Few crew members used them out of some sense of male pride. But I didn't want rust in my eyes. It was enough with rusty specks on my graying chest. After lunch, I took a brush and applied the initial anti-corrosive red paint. Later, we'd apply a yellow cover and finally a white surface coat. The men warned me to set a slow, steady pace. "This is a continuous task," they cautioned. "When we finish this deck, there is yet another. Then we begin all over again."

Rafael and deckhand Chino watched me while they chatted about films and women, especially mulatas. Like most Cubans, sailors tend to babble affectionately. They are sociable and give one another nicknames. The donkeyman is known as "philosopher" and "phenomenon," because he is witty and eats like a bear. Like the majority aboard, he is of mixed skin color. "Chino" is so named for his Asiatic eyes. In Cuba, it is not demeaning to give ethnic nicknames to people of mixed blood. Like seamen everywhere, Cuban sailors are frank, independent minded, stubborn, jokers and fun loving, and they complain a lot.

"Seamen would not be seamen if they didn't complain and poke fun." said Boatswain Ramiro.

Ramiro handed me a security belt to keep me from falling off the narrow ledge I was standing on to paint the deck's bulwark. When I finished that area, I joined Rafael and Chino on a scaffold made of splintered wood and rope. It was lowered down the hull at the forecastle. The hull must be treated the same as the decks: scraping oxidation, cleaning, sanding, painting three times. It was tricky painting the hull. Fourteen meters from water line to gunwale, we painted its length with a long-handled roller, called a "rocket", as we swung to and fro. My ass swayed all too close to the fetid muck. The painting motion was so tiring we took turns while one rested. When we took a longer break, we swung up the rope monkey-style to the gunwale. As I planted my feet hard on the deck, I felt sick from the putrid stench and spit in the mire. Havana harbor is said to be one of the world's foulest. Second only to Le Havre.

"Now, you're a real sailor," Ramiro said to me, all smiles, as I swung over the gunwale.

After chow, Ramiro decided to celebrate my initiation by taking me to port. Rafael and Zenia came along. We all wanted a drink or two but Havana harbor was no longer noted for its port life. There were only two places to drink that cater to sailors: Los Marinos Bar, on the corner of San Pedro at Santa Clara, and Bar Dos Hermanos, directly on the waterfront across from the launch stop and immigration checkpoint (6).

Los Marinos is a standup piloto bar, serving only rot-gut rum straight. Dos Hermanos is a hole-in-the-wall counter-bar, serving small glasses of tiny oysters and fish cocktails with its rum. Although it advertises for clams, it never has any and only sporadically does it have oysters. With the sale of fish or seafood snacks, it sometimes serves one glass of beer or a glass of Albanian or Bulgarian wine (until in the early `90s when Cuba's stock ran out and those countries' new capitalist economies ceased trading with Cuba). Sailors often gave away the food. They get enough food aboard ship but never enough booze.

Dos Hermanos closes when the food is consumed, and it was closed when we arrived. We were luckier at Los Marinos. Women rarely enter pilotos but exuberant Zenia fit right in. As we drank our rum, she told me of her life as a sailor.

Born in Havana, in 1948, she joined the merchant marines following the tenth congress of the CTC (7) when the trade unions opened more jobs to women, including a few positions on ships. Today women are allowed into more positions but there is no woman captain.

"In the beginning, some men had a hard time with women crew members," Zenia said, "but that wasn't the rule. Now, we're treated fine by all the men. There is no obligatory sex, although there is a good deal of flirtation and sexual joking, not to mention the act itself," she laughed.

The hefty woman felt fulfilled. She holds her own with the men, with their rough language and playful ways. Her cheeks puff up when she dishes out vulgarities as fluidly as her male colleagues. Nor is she offended when men gaze at her rolling buttocks and full-moon breasts.

"I have seen more of the world than I had ever dreamed before becoming a sailor. I earn more than doing comparable work ashore and life is more fun at sea. And, best of all, I have lots of friends."

Zenia's mother cared for her teenage son when she is sailing. Her son was studying to be a ship mechanic. Zenia had been divorced for several years and was content, "playing the field".

She recalled good times abroad and bad times, like when her ship caught fire in Canada due to someone carelessly soldering a lamp.

"We put out the fire without a great amount of damage, but it shocked the shit out of me. I even invoked Chango's name" (8).

Zenia, like most Cubans, is not a religious practitioner or thorough believer but she admires some rituals of Santería. And Zenia will admit that she practices some aspects, "just in case".

Rafael ordered more rum and joined the conversation.

"I don't agree. I think Cubans have always believed in something, be it religion, politics or leaders. And I believe in the 'evil forces'."

The "teacher" had his dark side, one that challenges the "evil forces".

"I love the sea for its magnetic force, its constant threat of danger. Its fearsomeness makes me feel alive. Once in Canada, our ship hit a cyclone; rather the cyclone hit us, right where the Atlantic meets gulf stream waters. It was fierce. We almost lost the ship and our lives. We all wore life jackets for days. There were other ships nearby, and some of their men were swept overboard. Nothing could be done during the entire five days we hung onto our lives by threads. We were all crying, I'll tell you that. And I prayed.

"I used to be a Baptist when I was a kid. I went to a private Baptist school before they were banned—or frowned upon. Then I got tired of Protestantism and switched to Catholicism. It was a child's fantasy: the whole idea of paradise and receiving Christ's blood. When I entered puberty, I stopped attending church. I had my first girl friend at 13. She had the movement and I had the motion. Her body fascinated me: the gyrations she made, the pleasure that oozed out of my penis. This made a greater impact on me than religion", said the handsome man, his mustache twitching.

"Then came the Young Communist Union and military service. I became serious while never neglecting the pleasurable sides of life. When the Communist party refused to accept my membership application—I was supposedly an 'intellectual' because I'd become a teacher and the party was then concentrating on recruiting the 'proletariat'—I gave up on politics and marxist studies. Today, I am a patriot and a revolutionary but I go my own way."

Rafael maintained his need "to believe in something". His mother is a medium. Her house in Vibora municipality has an extra bedroom where she holds spiritual sessions and tonques de santos. She and her husband, a foreign ministry diplomat, are revolutionaries and she sees no contradiction in celebrating gods and saints. The Communist party, with the forthright backing of Fidel, drew the same conclusion in its 1992 congress. Henceforth, all religious believers could become members.

"My mother and some friends influenced me and I began attending Santería services five years ago. Its mysticism gets to you, bit by bit. I can't explain what its structure and tenets are, not even to myself, but it is filled with legends and poetry that helps me find spiritual peace.

"Look, when you're at sea in a thunder storm it is comforting to call forth to Chango. I felt that Chango and Yemayá got me through that ghastly cyclone in Canada" (9).

Most sailors, religious or not, ideologists or uncommitted, are superstitious. It's in the nature of the work. In the end of my presence on the Shark, for instance, I acquired a reputation for bringing bad luck aboard because she never did get repaired while I was with her.

I wanted to see how a ship captain lived ashore, and what did a nationally renowned hero think of the "system"? Captain Urquiola drove me in his new Lada to his apartment building where he and his wife had a three-bedroom apartment, one of a dozen in a modern four-story building in Vedado. His wife, a short plump woman, had just returned from Villa Clara where she had attended her father's burial. She had made the same sad trip to her home province just two months before for her mother's funeral. Despite her personal losses, her drawn state, she managed to act the friendly hostess. Cookies, coffee and rum awaited us.

The Urquiolas lived alone in this brightly tiled and painted, comfortable apartment. They had running water and modern Cuban-made kitchen appliances. Their living conditions were what, perhaps, half the nation had, although they had more space than most. Their daughter had recently moved out with her husband. Her former bedroom served as Antonio's study.

The captain was in a garrulous mood.

"The revolution is stagnant and the people are impatient. If some major changes don't occur, I believe we'll have a social explosion. People lack the necessary incentive; they have no real participation or power at their work centers or in the society as a whole; they have nowhere to go with complaints or to demand change, to insist that revolutionary values be abided by. The power lies in the self-perpetuating, all-controlling Communist party.

"Cuba had its own genuine revolution, and has provided everyone with basic necessities. It has not been brutal like other socialist systems. But like any social system it must incorporate new ideas, new technology, and instill a dynamic, effective work ethic in the people.

"We can't always be blaming the Yankees for the things we lack. Why couldn't our agricultural workers and campesinos provide us with sufficient and varied foods? Why is the distribution system so lousy? Don't get me wrong. I don't want capitalism or multi-parties. I just want what we have to function efficiently so we all have enough. I want an economy and unions run by workers not bureaucrats and administrators appointed from above."

Captain Urquiola had refused to allow the party to bring in an outside functionary to head a CTC union aboard his ship.

"If the seamen want a union, fine, then they should select their spokesmen and arrange their own affairs."

Although the feisty captain convinced the party, the consequence was that there was no union aboard the Shark. This dilemma—worker-union power in relation to Communist party-government authority—was a current topic of national debate. There were varying viewpoints, such as we have heard from Captain Marrón and Seaweed seamen.

Urquiola believed that most young people are generally skeptical about the political system yet they lack the gumption to confront the wall that separates them from the decision-makers.

"Young people are spoiled on the one hand, and frustrated on the other. They are understandably anxious to be realized. Why can't they, for instance, travel abroad if they have the opportunity. Some do, some can't. Why? The government still doesn't routinely grant permission to travel. People don't possess their own passports. What is the government afraid of? Certainly a few travelers would stay abroad, but most would return after their eyes got accustomed to the new things they'd see. Maybe the party is afraid people with more knowledge would be more demanding. Regardless, it is absurd for us to be locked in."

Another test maneuver was scheduled the day after but when I arrived at port there were no launches. Ramiro came up beside me.

"There's nothing we can do, Ron. There is no petroleum for the launches, so they say. Our ship won't sail today with so many of us ashore. I'm going to the Caribe company store. Come along with me. Maybe we can get you a uniform."

As we strolled down narrow, cobble-stoned streets, one person after another pumped Ramiro's hand and patted his shoulders. He was greeted familiarly at the shipping company store, too. Ramiro asked for a pair of work boots for himself and a uniform for me. The shopkeeper took Ramiro's word that I was entitled to a uniform as an internationalist volunteer-trainee. The tan pants and shirt were attractive but cheaply made, as was the price: ten pesos. The shirt fit but the pants did not.

"Never mind," Ramiro said, "buy the suit and we'll exchange the pants at Mambisa's store. A bird in hand is worth a hundred flying."

We walked over to the other merchant marine shop where the shelves were empty. Ramiro was unperturbed. He whispered into the administrator's ear-ringed ear and the woman ducked behind a curtain. She returned carrying a pair of seaman's pants to fit. I had yet to earn the uniform as a seaman but I had done some on-the-job training as a participating journalist.

At Los Marinos a bartender was on duty to tell people no hay. Ramiro bent his ear and passed him a three-peso bill. The bartender ducked under the counter and produced two glasses with rot-gut rum. We downed them quickly, slapped backs and parted.

I hung around the wharf until a launch finally showed up. We made it to the Shark at the refinery dock but the captain was not aboard. He'd left instructions that we'd try again tomorrow.

Figure 10: A seaman painting "Shark", 1990.

Late next morning, the engine was cranked up and we sailed well enough for a few miles. I saw my favorite sea animal, the dolphin. A group of pico de botellas played at our bow. This species is exceptionally intelligent and gentle. Cuba has a special boat and crew to capture them for sale to European enterprises, which train them to perform in spectaculars.

Six miles north of Santa Maria del Mar, the helmsman spied two figures bobbing up and down on two huge tractor inner tubes tied together. The figures wore fatigues, Vietnamese-style straw hats, and they carried large knapsacks. They were not fishing. They were paddling north.

Captain Urquiola ordered the helmsman to circle them. The pair showed no indication that they wished to be assisted. As we got closer, I could make out facial features of a man in his 30s and a ruddy teenager. The youngster seemed a bit exhausted; the older man quite determined.

A couple seamen prepared to throw a life line but the chief engineer said it could be dangerous.

"The sea is choppy. They could slip trying to get into it and drown. They aren't in any trouble, not yet. Let's see what happens."

Some crewmen speculated that this was yet another couple hoping to reach international waters, 12 miles from shoreline and not far away, where they might get picked up by a foreign ship and taken to Miami. But the current was strong and darkness was approaching. These men risked joining the statistics of drowned persons who try but fail to enter the U.S. without a visa.

Figure 11: Coast guard picking up rafters headed towards Miami, 1990.

The United States had agreed with Cuba to annually admit up to 20,000 Cuban immigrants. Nevertheless, the US routinely denied visas to most applicants, admitting between five and 15% of their own quota. Cubans say that the US's logic in denying the quota, as well as denying legal entry for family visitations, is its, "Cynical encouragement to desperate persons to risk the perilous 'rush to freedom'."

When people attempt to cross the waters on shabby constructions, it bolsters the US posture that, "Cuba is a human rights abuser". And when some Cubans do reach United States shores, they are treated like heroes and given greater economic security than unemployed citizens.

Although Captain Urquiola believed in freedom to travel, he performed his duty and called the coast guard. The Shark continued circling the inner tubes as the older man, especially, continued paddling. An hour later, a coast guard boat sped up alongside the make-shift craft. A diver jumped into the water. He cut the inner tubes with a knife and assisted the two aboard the speed boat. The older man glared at him. The youngster looked tired and, perhaps, relieved.

The two security men and an armed soldier waved to our captain, who waved back without expression. The coast guard boat darted off toward shore.

The crew chattered about what they had just witnessed. Some thought it disgraceful that the pair sought to "abandon the fatherland", thus lending more propaganda ammunition for enemy assaults. Others emphasized the right to travel and the right to decide what to do with one's own life. Many valued the fact that the pair "tienen cojones" (10). Some commented that they were crazy from both political and nationalist perspectives and the danger involved. Within a couple hours, winds blew strongly and swelled the sea to three-meter heights.

The captain told me he'd only followed instructions, but had also done so, "because they deserved to be saved from drowning".

Despite the Communist party-led government's lack of priority for and guarantees of civil liberties—especially public debate with opposition to Fidel, free press and free travel—I rarely encounter a Cuban who is afraid to speak his/her mind. On the contrary, people are quite opinionated and more than willing to effuse their criticisms of the system, of Fidel, of anything, while most of those who criticize—just like Captain Urquiola and Sigi—are quite proud to be Cuban and to be part of the revolution, whether they believe it is dying or not. Most people are not afraid to be punished for their opposition to policy. What I witnessed in the debate about "freedom of travel", including defections to the enemy, is a good example of this. Here we had some deckhands and mechanics differing with their more critical captain, and they did so in his presence. Nor was he afraid that a zealot Communist member—he was also a member—would squeal on him to some bureaucrat.

After a night rolling up and down choppy waves, the chief engineer informed the captain that the engine was stilling malfunctioning. We limped back to port. I packed my bags and told Captain Urquiola that I simply had to sail. He said he'd talk to the administration about finding me a navigable ship. A week later, we met at the company office. I'd been speedily granted the request; I'd be sailing with Seaweed in a few days. The captain had good news too.

"I'm off the fucking Rumala, Ron," he nearly sang, his face beaming for the first time in those six weeks I'd spent with him.

"Seguridad finally cleared me to travel abroad, and Mambisa just gave me a cargo ship. See you at sea, my man!"

A few days later, scuttle butt had it that Captain Urquiola had set off for Mexico with dry cargo. Rumor also had it that the pair of would-be defectors had merely been fined for the crime of "illegal exit", and released.

Notes:

1. Urquiola's role is briefly portrayed in my 1991 book. He was one of the 26 Cuban and one Italian moles who came out of the cold in July 1987.

2. Security, another name for DSE.

3. Cuba's general defense strategy was established in 1981 with the aid of Vietnamese military advisors. It is based on millions of trained militia to protect their home areas while the military is readied to fight on battle fronts.

4. A mild Mexican profanity.

5. A stronger Cuban profanity, taking strength from seven-year rum.

6. Sailors Bar and Two Brothers Bar.

7. Central de Trabajadores (Central Organization of Cuban Trade Unions).

8. Chango is a key saint in the Afro-Cuban Santería religion, which stems from the Yoruba people—Western African coastal people—and their language. He is their animist god of fire, thunder and lightning. He is mighty and a demanding lover. His role is similar to many pre-monotheistic cultures, such as in the Nordic countries with Thor, their god of the same elements.

9. Yemayá is the Virgin of Regla, mother of life and the queen of the seas, which flow from her womb. Regla is also the name given to a municipality across the bay in eastern Havana where the main church has a statute of the black virgin holding a white Jesus. The story is that the all-powerful Yoruba god, Olofi, shaped Yemayá from fire and rock and she became the first god of earth. A virtuous mother, she is also gay and alluring and has possessed many male saints. Yemayá enjoys undulating and agitating dances. She is particularly close to Ochún, the sexiest of saints, to whom she gave the rivers to rule. Yemayá, quite naturally, is the protector of seamen. See my poem, Cuba: Tenacious Royal Palm, about Chango and Ochún, in the appendix.

10. They have balls.

CHAPTER SIX: GIORITA:
Sailing to Europe

Figure 12: Giorita on way to Holland from Cuba, 1992.

Three luggage bags, a large cardboard box of books and papers, and a straw trunk sit on the ground before the gate. My trusty European bicycle rests against the restraining wire. A Nicaraguan leather brief case and canvas camera bag hand over my shoulders; a backpack on my back. I hold my typewriter case in one hand; I grasp documents granting me permission to sail with Giorita from Mambisa and two ministries in my other.

A customs official takes my papers and reads them.

"Where is the permission to sail from the port authority?"

I knew it. I told you so, Ron. No, don't worry. The Mambisa agency man told me the permission would be at the customs gate office. You can count on it, he said.

"Compañero, Mambisa personnel told me the port authority would have signed the request to sail and that it would be here. Please look amongst your papers."

He shuffles through papers on his desk.

"There is nothing here in your name. You can't leave the wharf without permission to sail and Major Madrón is the only man to grant permission. He won't be back until tomorrow. That's the way it is."

I see the ship's anchors lifting. I scream.

Red Tape.

I awoke in a sweat. No, it won't be like that, not this time, I assured myself. Today, I am supposed to board the ship I have been assigned. The process to get to this point had taken ten weeks. I had visited six offices in two ministries, the Central Committee and the Mambisa shipping company a total of 53 times; talked with 21 people in person and a score more over the telephone.

Many Cubans have told me of similar experiences when about to travel. They are sometimes stopped from boarding a flight when they are to attend conferences or cultural events as participants. Even well known musicians or representatives of cultural and social institutions have had their travel papers delayed to the point of missing the plane and thus the event where they were to represent Cuba. I could understand or rationalize—given the nature of reality: the constant United States sabotage against the country's leaders and its economy—that the Ministry of Interior had an impossible job: to balance the real objectives of national security (the security of its people, thousands of whom had been killed or injured by U.S. saboteurs) and the interests of freedom to travel, even to represent the nation's society. In the final analysis, it is MININT which allows Cubans, or residents such as myself, to exit the country. Their concern is: can this person harm us abroad? If so, how? Should we allow him or her to leave and possibly do us damage?

I'd gone through a lot of bureaucratic battles but this one had been the worst. After working three years at Editorial José Martí my final contract ran out. The publishing house was cutting back, like all others, and I was on poor terms with the director—who later was fired for incompetence. It was time to get a new job or return to Denmark. I did not want to leave Cuba nor did I want to lose Grethe. We had not had the close marriage we'd enjoyed the first year or two but we still loved each other. I sought to maintain our marriage as well as my connection to Cuba. Solidarity committees in Europe and Los Angeles arranged for me to hold talks about Cuba in their countries and to sell my book, "Backfire", and others by Cubans. I wanted to sail across the Atlantic on a Cuban ship. It would be cheaper than flying and allow me to take excess weight, especially many books and notes, which I needed for my writings. My primary reason for sailing was to write about the experience. This would fill out a book I would write about voyaging with Cuban tankers and a cargo ship, a unique setting in which to see Cubans. I looked forward to a few months away in which I could be with Grethe, write this book and represent Cuba to audiences in several countries. I could then return with a book in hand and take on an offer to write for new tourist and medical publications. In that way, I could help the economy, earn a living and feel that I was doing something positive. Cuba had no passenger ships, nor did foreign passenger ships stop in Cuba. But once in a while, a Cuban cargo ship would take on a Cuban passenger to facilitate that person's work, which was usually connected to some state mission. The shipping company knew me so it was worth a try.

This is my story of the process.

I cycled to Mambisa. I knew the sub-director slightly. He was on leave. A substitute listened enthusiastically to my story and proposal. He said that the practice of allowing a passenger was exceptional but possible. There were even forms and set fares. He told me to leave references and return in a week. The following week, Mambisa's director, Osvaldo Calero, had approved my request. So fast. I was elated. The substitute sub-director added that I "merely" had to go to the foreign relations department of the Ministry of Transportation (MINTRANS) where I would be investigated. They would then send their recommendation to Mambisa's director. The whole process should take two weeks.

At MINTRANS, the man in charge said that was not the procedure. First, Mambisa's director must write a letter and a form must be filled out explaining the purpose of my "mission".

I returned to Mambisa's sub-director's substitute. He didn't know that procedure. I should wait a few days; the director to take care of this. The following week, I was told that Director Calero had written the letter and that it had been sent to MINTRANS.

"In your case, the letter did not go through intermediary channels but was sent directly to the vice-minister in charge of international relations. The form had not been properly filled out and is being redone. Try next Friday," I was told. I felt quite impressed with their confidence in me.

I figured it was wise to see the vice-minister and let him know some of my background before he evaluated my case. Otherwise he might send the matter elsewhere. The vice-minister was unavailable but his assistant saw me. The elder military man took detailed notes of my request and I left with him what documentation I had. He'd see to it that the vice-minister would read my request. I should return on Monday. When I appeared I was told that the vice-minister had been out of the office but his assistant had news. The head of international relations' decision was that he could make no decision.

"You must get initial permission from the Communist party's Central Committee."

I threw up my hands and turned on my heels.

Daunted yet determined, I cycled to the Central Committee (CC) and chained my iron horse to the barricaded boundary and walked up to a white-gloved guard. He took my name and called to someone. He then waved me through. The CC is one of three large buildings behind the tall José Martí statute at the Revolutionary Square. Inside the marbled lobby, I asked to speak to the person-in-charge of such matters. A secretary said that would be the organizing secretary, one of the nation's top leaders. He had just taken a leave of absence, in order to do voluntary agricultural work for two weeks. I explained my situation. The secretary took this quite naturally and said I should type a letter of request, which she would deliver to him.

Disheartened again, I cycled home and wrote the letter. Back at the CC, the secretary assured me that her boss would see to it when he returned. I had to wait.

I returned in two weeks.

"Yes, the Central Committee approves your request," the secretary told me, cheerfully. "I'll call MINTRANS about this. Don't worry," she encouraged.

That's Cuba. When you least expect success, what you've been seeking comes through for you, and usually at the last minute. It feels like "they" know when they've put you through the wringer enough and now it's time to deliver. But wait, Ron. You know better than to count your chickens before they hatch.

At MINTRANS, I was told that the vice-minister was on vacation for two weeks. Or was it two weeks volunteer work? I asked to see the minister. He wasn't in. His secretary saw me instead. Yes, they had received a phone call from CC. "Go see Mambisa's dispatcher and he'll process getting you a ship."

I rushed to Mambisa's office where I got to see the dispatcher.

"Yes, I understand. Fine. All I need is something in writing confirming this," the dry dispatcher replied, as if he'd seen saying that all his life.

"In writing? The Central Committee did not say anything about that. Besides, you know a man as busy and important as the organizing secretary is not going to write anything about one passenger on a ship."

"Yes, well, I'm sorry. I have my instructions. I must have written confirmation. I'll call his assistant about it. Please give me the numbers," he said, softening up a bit.

"Sure. I'll give them to you but you know it is very difficult to get through."

Feeling certain that the Mambisa dispatcher would not be persistent enough to accomplish the task, I biked to MINTRANS. I asked to see their dispatcher so that he could pressure Mambisa's dispatcher to do the job. MINTRANS' dispatcher, Silvio, was a graduate from a Canadian university. He'd recently earned a doctorate in "management decision-making". Boy, was that something this outfit needed, I thought.

Silvio heard my tale and smiled.

"Look, give me 24 hours to straighten out this mess. This is a simple passenger matter, not anything that should involved top leadership."

YOU said it.

"Call me tomorrow. There'll be no problems. Don't worry."

When anyone in a government office tells me not to worry that's just what I do.

"I'll come by. It's easier."

Instead of waiting, I went to see the CC secretary. I actually got to see the top man's assistant.

"Don't worry, Ron. You'll make the trip. We have nothing against it; we want you to go," he said, congenially.

"Good. But why does this Mambisa dispatcher tell me he can't do anything until he has something in writing from the Central Committee?"

"I called the minister's office and they said it was OK without a letter," the assistant said.

"Yeah, they told me the same thing. But the Mambisa dispatcher is the real power guy because he is the implementer and he insists on a signed paper."

"Listen, Ron, I'll take care of it. Don't worry."

These guys don't want to put anything in writing. But why? Can it be a matter of "covering ass"?

The next day, Silvio wasn't in. I tried three times. The following day I got to see Silvio. He said he'd talked to the Mambisa dispatcher.

"Everything will be fine. You shouldn't have to go to all these offices," he said. "Mambisa's dispatcher is instructed to take care of your passage."

Once again I cycled to Mambisa. This time the dispatcher's face was more uptight than ever.

"Listen, I still have to have something in writing. I know we have too much bureaucracy, too much paperwork. But that's the way it is!"

I couldn't restrain myself any longer.

"Your ministry's vice-minister, its dispatcher, Mambisa's own director, and the assistant to the Central Committee's organizing secretary all tell me that permission is granted and that you know this and that you should begin the process of finding me a ship. Why don't you just do it?"

"I will call you when I have some news," the dispatcher maintained firmly.

In the course of the next two weeks, I learned that Mambisa's dispatcher had tried to reach the CC assistant but never found him in. I went to the Ministry of Foreign Relations and got the head of the International Press Center to write a recommendation for me that maybe could help. At least I had something in writing. I didn't get to see MINTRANS' new "management decision-making" expert again. Silvio's 24 hours had come and gone many times. He was probably as irritated with the inflexibility of red tape as I and was embarrassed to see me. I was an unpleasant reminder of reality. My pertinacious characteristic had almost always brought me reprobation, and so it would. Despite personal censure I would persist. The "mission"—be it a personal yet honest one or one I believed to be in the common interest, a righteous one (or, as some would say, self-righteous)—propelled me to act until successful or until it was clear to me that no matter what I did I would fail.

Experience had taught me not to rely on people's good will. I would always hear that, yes, he or she would call, or write a letter, or whatever. That almost never occurred. But in this long process, I did receive three phone calls. The last one was from the CC assistant who told me not to pay for an air flight, which I had finally decided to do and had told him so. "The letter is on the way."

That day I checked in at Mambisa for what I hoped would be the last time. Lo and behold! Director Calero stood before his office door and greeted me.

"Ah, yes, Ron, glad to meet you. I am sorry for all the trouble you have been put through. But now it is all over. Your trip is approved."

My heart beat fast. But I had heard this before. In fact, as you may recall, he had been the first to "approve" my trip in the first days of my solicitude.

"Be so kind as to return tomorrow and the sub-director of exploitation will start the process to find a ship to Europe on which you may sail."

The next day, I learned that, indeed, the sub-director did what was promised. He assigned me to a captain whose task was to find such a ship. He had more rank than a dispatcher, that's for sure. There was no ship ready for Europe that week. Two weeks later, the sub-director told me that the Giorita would soon be sailing to Rotterdam and I could sail with her. He told me I could pay my passage at a particular office. Here I met the charming clerk in charge, Aurora, and paid 408 pesos. This included meals. She gave me a receipt and a LETTER for Giorita's captain. I had my first letter! Infatuated, I invited her for a drink. She agreed to meet me and we made love afterwards.

It was that night in which I had the nightmare.

The next morning, haggard from the nightmare but still exhilarated from a night of rigorous romance, I cycled to customs and immigration offices—the final step. The Mambisa LETTER and payment receipt, as well as MININT's permission to leave the country, did the trick. The customs and immigration people told me they would check my baggage 48 hours before sailing. Armed with my documentation, I biked several kilometers to where the Giorita was docked. She looked marvelous. She was still being unloading from her previous trip. The captain wasn't aboard so I waited in the recreation salon and browsed through the library. There were political books mixed with novels, even some by favorite authors, such as: Sinclair Lewis, Sherwood Anderson and John Reed, and many classic Russian novels.

A short, middle-aged, serious-looking man walked in. I introduced myself to Captain Carlos García González. He took my LETTER.

"Impossible! I'm full up. This ship is limited to 32 persons and I've got 32 officers and men."

Permission my ass. Permission does not matter if no one takes the captain into consideration. You can imagine how I felt. Yet I also knew that when it comes to the crunch there is more often than not a last minute solution.

The captain was frowning and puffing a bit. He held a bike pump.

"I see you cycle as well, captain," I said, as calmly as possible. "I have had my bike 12 years. Brought it all the way from Denmark and I'd planned to take it back with me on this trip. You see, I have so much stuff to carry I can't possibly go by plane. And I'm going to write a book and have so many notes..."

"Come to my cabin and let's talk," he said, interested.

I methodically counted 56 stairs up to his cabin. He introduced me to his wife, his son-in-law and two meteorologists, one of whom was to take the next voyage for training. Captain García sat behind his large desk and phoned Mambisa. I looked at the spacious and well kept living quarters while I waited, trying to appear calm.

As the phone rang, the captain spoke to me.

"I feel badly for you. It's not your fault, but they should consult the captain on these matters. I just can't take on a passenger when there is no space."

"Yes, I quite understand," I replied, expectantly.

While we waited, the meteorologists asked me about my planned trip. When I got to the point that I would be writing a book about sailing and that this trip would form the last chapter, the captain looked up.

"You mean you would write about the Giorita?"

"Certainly. That is part of my purpose."

"Do you play chess?"

"Yes."

"That does it! You're going even if I have to take two men off the manifest to make room."

"Surely there must be some other way," I replied with joy and reservation. "I could sleep in a cabin for two and I could work as well."

"No. It is more important that you write. You come aboard in two days with your stuff and we'll have a cabin for you. Don't worry about the customs and immigration check. They are closed on the weekends, and when plans are changed and you don't get informed until the last minute then you are not to blame, nor am I. So you just come directly to ship with your belongings."

At that point, the Mambisa man came on the other end of the line.

A colleague drove me and my stuff to the dock on Sunday. As it turned out no member of the crew was dislodged but the meteorologist would not be accompanying us. The ship's itinerary was: Cienfuegos, Barcelona, Amsterdam, Felixstowe, Montreal and return. I would depart at Amsterdam. There were loading delays so I had time to deliver my plants to a neighbor and say final farewells. Two days later, I boarded Giorita. The cabin I was given had a modern bathroom with shower and the living quarters were double the size I was used to on tankers. Plenty of room for my bike. There was even a desk where I placed my portable typewriter and notes for future writing.

Many say: "The system doesn't work; too much correcorre" (1). Like most things in peoples' lives it works and it doesn't work, and whichever way "it" goes there is an uplifting magical realism to it all (if you go with the flow).

Havana-Cienfuegos

I explored the ship while stevedores loaded about 500 containers. The 147 meter-long, 20 meter-wide vessel could carry 712 containers, each weighing about two tons empty and up to 22 tons when loaded. We were to collect the remaining containers in Cienfuegos. Giorita was one of three Chinese ships, all of the same make, Cuba bought in 1988. With a deadweight of 12,000 tons and maximum displacement of 18,000, the Giorita barely fits into the category of a large ship. First named Sierra Maestra, she got her named changed when registered in Cyprus as a demise charter. No one aboard knew what Giorita signified.

The stevedores were stacking containers eight levels high—five below deck and three above, reaching nearly to the bridge. The ship had nine decks. Stacking containers is a skill that requires utmost attention. They must be placed to maintain balance, and in such a way that they can be unloaded in the order of ports to visit. It is difficult work, even more so when there is no uniform weight to the cargo in the containers, as was the case on this voyage. In Havana harbor, as in most ports in the world today, gigantic wharf cranes lift the containers and lower them in place. Each ship carries two to five cranes (Giorita had two) used when port cranes are broken or nonexistent.

I looked about the interior as loading continued. The cleanliness of the ship impressed me most, a glaring contrast to grimy tankers. The chamber maids keep the rooms well swept, vacuumed and moped. Soap and polish were also in use. Captain García was known for cleaning his own carpets. The cabins, corridors, and mess halls were all attractively decorated with landscape paintings. In addition to paintings, the recreation room had a color television with video, and a domino table. The bridge was equipped with modern electronic technology, including: echo sounder (replaced sonar), chronometer, direction finder and satellite (which fixes location), weather satellite, telegraph-radio console, wind direction indicator, climometer, smoke detector and two atlas electronic radars.

Each crew member had his or her own cabin; many contained a small refrigerator. Some officers had two-room cabins. One was the purser, who was also the nurse. The doctor maintained dispensary and hospital rooms with essential medicines. The doctor on this trip was Galinda. She showed me what she had to use: oxygen, heat treatment lamp, mobile hospital bed, elementary surgical equipment and two refrigerators. Galinda was 44 years-old and had sailed for years. She told me that after the collapse of Comecon Cuba was the only nation remaining which required a doctor to be aboard on long-distance voyages. No Cuban ship sails anywhere without at least a trained nurse aboard. Other countries rely on officers' first aid training.

The most common medical problems are: cuts and bruises, foreign objects in eyes, muscle spasms, asthma, diabetes, hypertension, the common cold and bronchitis. Galinda makes regular checkups on each tour, especially on those with a chronic illness, and she sews many stitches.

"There is no doubt about it. If we didn't have doctors aboard more crew members would die. I cared for a man once who had a massive heart attack. He was immensely fat. Unfortunately, he died. But on other occasions, I've been able to give successful emergency treatment to men with appendicitis and other organ failures until we could get them to a hospital."

The engine room was also clean. There was not even any litter in one's path. The control room was all electronic. Like most equipment in the wheelhouse, the switch board was made by Germany's Siemens corporation. Even the ship's design was German. The only recognizable Chinese ingredient was the manufacturer plaque put up by the Sulz shipping company.

"The construction and design of container ships is international," the second engineer explained. "Most container ships look pretty much the same. Our engine is Japanese made, for example, but assembled in China. The hull and valves were made in China, but most parts and machinery come from many other countries."

Modesto, a farmer turned seaman, was the chief engineer. He showed me the 7,800-horse power, six-cylinder engine.

"This is a fine engine with a maximum speed of 17 knots. We usually sail between 13 and 14 depending on the winds. The only problem is its cylinder liners. It seems there is a manufacture defect, which causes the liners to crack. Neither we nor the manufacturers can find out why. Cuba and the manufacturer share the costs of replacing the liners. Each liner costs $25,000. We have spent several hundreds of thousands of dollars on this problem in just four years time. And the other two Chinese ships we bought have been docked for two years because we can't afford the repairs. We might get the problem resolved now that Japanese representatives have been here and promised to put in a whole new cylinder liner system at their expense.

"I've sailed on ships built by many other companies. The best ships that Cuba has bought are those six from Denmark built for us in the 1970s. I've sailed with them, including a cargo ship used for training. They never suffer breakdowns. They are excellently built; the only ships that never give us engine problems."

Modesto oversaw four machinists, three oilers, an electromechanic, electrician, turner and a student. The captain had direct charge of three bridge officers, an officer student, a radio operator and doctor. The boatswain oversaw the work of three helmsmen and three deckhands. The purser was in charge of two cooks and two chamber maids.

The crew earned five to six percent more than cabotaje crews, because they spend so much of their lives sailing long distances. Each member earned an additional $2 daily when sailing. The ship might make four or five trips annually, usually to and fro Europe, but most crew members made three trips a year and had four months free.

"Ay, caramba! I wish we'd leave and get it over with," exclaimed Ramón, the third machinist. "All these delays. I hate it this time of year. I never get used to the bad weather period. I've been in enough cyclones this time of year. The ship tilts and sways all the time. I get dizzy. I can't eat. I feel like I want to die. I wish we'd get it over with."

Departure time came and went and was reestimated three times. We spent a lot of time watching television, which broadcast that three cyclones were surging over the Atlantic. We didn't sail the following day either. We were three days behind schedule when the last containers were loaded. It was a varied cargo: bull horns and toe nails for an Amsterdam decorative business, shirts and towels, plasterboards made from sugar cane, molasses, metal scrap, and children's books.

The chief in charge of loading, Juan Carlos, told me what caused the delays.

"Under optimal conditions, we can load 250 empty containers or 150 filled ones in a long day. But we always have problems these days in getting enough fuel to run tractor-trailers. Another problem was that this brigade was not well coordinated."

The wharf crane was now hoisting pallets loaded with our food supply: six large sea bass, several groupers and hundreds of smaller fish; 18 sides of pork (nine whole pigs), hundreds of chickens, slabs of beef; sacks of potatoes, sweet and malanga, packages of rice, white-brown-black beans, onions, garlic, butter, 20 huge crates of eggs, scores of cartons of Cuba's best coppelia ice cream...

There was enough food for the crew for two months, food for hot meals with meat or fish, plus soups with meat, root and green vegetables twice a day, and two snacks daily.

After chow, customs and immigrations officials boarded to check passports and for stowaways. No one checked my luggage, just as the captain had predicted. The pilot arrived and the departure maneuver began. I watched from the bow as we sidled out. Mooring lines were still newly white and unfrayed. Bitts and windlass were freshly painted. No oil, grease or rust spotted the deck.

Once again I was sailing past the Morro Castle. The water was choppy. Lightning struck and the ship vibrated. Contrasting emotions quivered within me. Uplifted was the strongest sensation I felt later in the captain's cabin. As the clock struck midnight on October first, he and a handful of the men toasted my 53rd birthday.

Heavy weather hit us in the predawn hours. Steel doors banged open and shut. The ship shook, rattled and rolled, tossing me about in bed. Music blared from somewhere on an upper deck. I rolled out of bed and dressed. I had to find the source of noise or I could not sleep. I traced the static to an outside speaker hanging above a banging door. I asked the officer on bridge watch how to turn it off. He said the control was in the telegraph room. Pedro, the radio operator, was still on duty waiting weather warnings. He turned the outside speaker off and asked me to stay awhile.

Pedro was only 42 years old but his black skin was already set off with silver-gray chest hairs. He sat bare-chested before a large Japanese radio console. The wireless telegraph received and transmitted telephone and Morse code messages anywhere in the world, on water and land. A JAX-19 facsimile for receiving weather reports sat across the room. Static began squawking out of the radio console, followed by dots and dashes. Pedro flipped the Morse code handle for several minutes as rapidly as fingers can move. He didn't take one note, and sometimes spoke to me while he listened to or sent a communication. Pedro explained that he sums up in his head the dots and dashes into words, "reading" the message as it comes in. He then sends his message, letter by letter, without needing to write the words beforehand.

"It's all up here in my curly, white-haired head," the 26-year veteran seaman said.

I returned to my cabin and fell into a fitful half-sleep. By dawn, the sea had swollen and doors were still banging. Rain was falling. Winds were at 30 knots. We were in a minor tropical storm with whitecaps two meters high spraying over the sea. Our instruments indicated we were sailing in six to seven Beaufort scale conditions. No one worked on deck until we reached Cienfuegos.

I was again awakened by noise on our second night out. This time it was a whining alarm. I put on my shorts and rushed to the bridge to learn that it was a false alarm.

"Someone was smoking too near a smoke detector," Raúl, the second mate, replied to my inquiry. "Detectors are very sensitive," the bespeckled man added, blowing smoke through his nose.

We arrived at Cienfuegos the following morning. Although we only had 212 containers to load, we would be there four days. The dock supervisor was rarely present to coordinate the work. I watched with dismay as stevedores haggled over where to place the containers. The tractor-trailer driver engaged his clutch forward, then backward as loaders shouted conflicting instructions.

On the third morning, the captain wrote on the departure blackboard that we would leave at 15:00.

"We're leaving today for sure," Captain García told me over coffee. "This is the worst ever. The workers just don't want to work."

"Well, it is the weekend," I responded, not wanting to sound my usual pessimistic self.

"It's always the weekend!" Captain García said, disgustedly, and left.

Alberto shook his bushy, white hair.

"There is no work discipline," the seaman sighed.

Gallardo, a short helmsman, defended the stevedores.

"The Torricelli embargo makes our situation all the more difficult. The United States tightens its blockade. We receive less and less petroleum. Foreign ships trading with us can't dock in US ports for six months if they dock here. Do you really think these workers don't want this ship to leave at the very first hour possible?"

"I don't think that they think one bit about when this ship sails. They get the same wages and benefits whether they load one container or the quota of 250 per shift. Workers have too many rights, especially the right not to work," quipped Alberto.

"What the hell does the Torricelli law, or the 'Cuban Democracy Act' as they misname it, have to do with indolence?" I put in. "It is past time to blame poor work on the blockade. The state tells us that we have to fight the Yankee blockade with greater work discipline. But no one intervenes to facilitate effective work. People should insist that the government, and the party, permit significant worker impute in the decision-making process. That might help produce effective work."

It took the brigade of six stevedores five more hours to load the remaining 12 containers. Alberto inspected the bolts and bars that secure the containers. He told the head stevedore and the watch officer that the latchings were loose. The stevedore shrugged his shoulders. The officer went to see the captain.

Alberto showed me the bars and cables. They flipped easily when touched.

"This is deadly for the cargo and for us," Alberto said, sadly. "I was on a run recently from Spain to Italy when bad weather hit. Seven containers near the bow broke out of the latches and fell into the sea. They hadn't been tightened properly. Fortunately, they were empty. Had they been filled, their weight could have toppled others, like a house of cards, and the ship could have lost balance and tilted over."

Thank Yemayá for that non-fatal accident.

"The stevedores have not spent the necessary time and care to secure the latches. Now, we'll have to wait until tomorrow to sail," Alberto concluded.

I asked Gallardo how he viewed the situation.

His lips pursed, his eyes squinted. He removed his brimmed combatant cap and slowly searched for a place to put it down. Finding none, he slapped it back on his head. The veteran Communist cleared his throat and looked straight at the quay.

"These stevedores are Revolutionaries. Communists. Patriots. Good workers. But they have problems just like everyone else. Their working conditions are not optimal. They lack fuel to haul the containers. They have to leave the job-site to eat lunch. It is Sunday and they want to be with their families. They didn't tighten the latches sufficiently for these reasons not because they don't care. Moreover, these workers are not specialized in latching down, and this load is not a priority, otherwise they would have worked quicker and the coordinator would have found latching experts," he concluded, grinding his teeth.

I found the captain in his cabin, manipulating his computer-video keyboard. Blip, blip sounded the animated robot as it shoveled up bullets.

"Are we staying the night?" I asked.

"Yep." His eyes remained fixed on the game. "What a waste of time and money. It only takes Barcelona stevedores one day to handle 600 containers. But there is nothing to do about this."

On our fourth day in port, the stevedores managed to tighten the latches by noon. As we prepared for departure, a bevy of wives and girl friend visitors climbed down the gangway. We sailed away from Cuba as the sun was setting on October 5. I felt a personal loss due to the delay. I would miss the Belgium congress on Cuba where I was to speak. But that was nothing, not compared to the three days wasted in which Cuba could have earned vital income with the use of one of their ships.

The Long Voyage

I spent the first evening pestering the first and second mates for data about our cargo and route. We were carrying a light load: only 1,158 tons of merchandise. Counting the ship's own weight, fuel, fresh water and ballast sea water, the crew's weight and its food, it weighed 12,000 tons, 6,000 tons under capacity—a sign of the rough economic times for Cuba.

Second mate Raúl, who was the navigator, punched figures into his hand calculator.

"If the captain maintains the same course—round Cabo Cruz direct to Windward Pass and into the Atlantic, hugging the north coast of Haiti, in order to miss a cyclone predicted for the normal route, then northeast towards the Azores, then due east into the Strait of Gibraltar, then across the Mediterranean to Barcelona—it should take 14 days and 15 hours, a total of 4,567 nautical miles. That is, if we average 13 knots, which is routine during the windy winter weather. Then it is 1,941 miles, or 6 days and two hours, to Amsterdam. Your voyage will take 22 days, depending on how many hours we have in Barcelona, and the ever-unpredictable winds."

I chatted with Raúl when he finished charting the rest of the ship's route to England and Montreal and return to Cuba (total time away would be a calculated 42 days).

Raúl was raised on or near the sea. His grandfather, father and uncle had been or still were merchant marines. As a young man, Raúl had joined the revolution to overthrow Batista. He enlisted in the merchant marines soon after the triumph. Now 56 years old, he'd been sailing for 27 years and he looked older.

On a voyage to southern Africa, Raúl had worked on a refrigerated ship and experienced frequent and drastic shifts in temperature, from 35-40 degrees to minus 25 degrees. One ear was ruptured and he lost the hearing in that ear as a consequence of these sudden changes.

"A sailor's life is hard. I feel tired. I look forward to retirement. Fortunately, our government has an early retirement plan so I can retire in four years. I can't complain about my daily life. It is very routine. My body is so accustomed to the same watch shifts that it hardly feels it is navigating. And my life is more tranquil since I've been married to Luz. We've sailed together most of our marriage, 12 years now. We have separate cabins and distinct work hours. She works the day and I work all hours. We don't sleep together much but we go back and forth to each other's cabins when we like. We are content.

"We don't go out much when ashore. We prefer to enjoy our home and each other's company. We read, watch television and sail together. That's our life. And we are not jealous people like many others. We don't fear we will cheat on each other, even when we have to be separated because there is no need for both of us on a particular voyage. No one on this ship makes passes at Luz. This is a stable, respectful crew. The captain is reliable and insists on reliability from everyone."

I was impressed by a modern 10-gear bicycle propped up against a cloth-covered sofa in Raúl's cabin. He had bought it in Canada for his wife. The two-room cabin was decorated with large photos of Fidel, Che, Camilo Cienfuegos and Celia Sanchéz. The door opened and Luz walked in. The shy woman nodded hello and sat down on the sofa. She was one of the two stewards and the current destacada worker. It was said that it was her Chinese blood that made her exceptionally rapid and efficient in her work.

"I was working in a factory when I read an announcement on the bulletin board encouraging women to join the merchant marines," Luz explained how she became a sailor 15 years ago.

"I was 30 years old, still single and with no children. I had a good friend whose husband was a purser. He encouraged me to apply. It sounded interesting and it was work the government had use for. So I signed up. I never thought I'd stay. But here I am," she grinned.

Not now as shy as usual, Luz continued her story.

"I had never been on a ship before but I soon got used to the strange motions. I learned to like navigating. It is stable and tranquil—most of the time. I've never met catastrophically bad weather. There are no big problems or daily annoyances when sailing: no long lines, no crowded buses, no correcorre. I feel relaxed. Sometimes we're gone for several months. We get to see new places, new faces. I've enjoyed all this with my husband for most of our 12 years together.

"I met Raúl aboard ship. We started a romance and got married a year later. It's been a good marriage sailing together. I wouldn't want to be married to a sailor if I were not sailing with him. One misses too much of life if you are separated a lot. It's best to be with someone. Isn't that why we married?"

Raúl agreed.

"Luz and I are planning to spend part of our next vacation at a campsite for volunteer agricultural workers. We enjoy working the fields. It is a pleasant distraction from the routine at sea, and is another facet of life that we share."

For the next two days, we sailed down Cuba's western coast, passing the Sierra Maestras and then along the southern coastline. Fortunately, we were too far out to see the hated Yankee naval base, which they call Guantánamo after the province from which they stole the area. I had visited the province and came as close to the military base as possible on the Cuban controlled side. I could see uniformed figures through a telescope on top of a lookout post. I gave them The Finger out of anger and impotence at their rapacious, occupationist behavior.

Soon we were sailing through the Windward Passage. We could see villages on the Haitian coast for several hours. Then there was nothing to see except the world's second largest bodies of water, the Atlantic. The Pacific is twice its size. It would be ten days before we would sight land again.

The captain had us practice drills for fire and ship abandonment. Wilfredo, the third mate, showed me how to board the enclosed lifeboat with life vest in hand. The boat is built for 32. My seat was located at the bow, number 31. The lifeboat was cabled to the poop deck below the smoke stack upon which was painted Mambisa's logo: a fist gripping a machete with a big red star over it. It was forceful but I wondered why a machete would be a tool used to symbolize seamen's' work.

On the fourth day out, we sailed through the first of six invisible time zones we would pass. Now I divided my time by getting to know the rest of the crew and observe work operations. I also began writing about my tanker experiences in the most perfect of settings: rhythmically swaying in tune with lapping waves under my spacious berth. After my work day, I would take a swim in the pool. After a sumptuous dinner, I would read or watch a video with others. Sometimes I would play the national "indoor" game, dominos, which was the men's favorite pastime.

The captain insisted upon strict discipline throughout the ship. The rules and duties, in fact, were observed. I would come to know the crew to be skilled and serious people, respectful of one another and the captain. One of his rules was no drinking, except when he specifically permitted group drinking in limited amounts. During the month I was with him there was only one such occasion.

Captain Carlos García González sat as his desk in shorts. His T-shirt slipped up his midriff when he laughed, which he often did when playing video-computer games with the purser and doctor.

"He never loses nor can he tolerate to lose, just like a little boy," Galinda said tenderly of him.

I asked the captain why he was so strict about drinking, what his views were on sailing, about Cuba and the world's problems. The gallego (2) was in a garrulous mood. He began speaking with his feet resting on his tidy desk and gradually straightened as his sociological wisdom came through.

"I've been a seaman for 28 years; a captain since I was 27. I'm 49 now, so for 22 years I've been a captain. I have learned that the men must be alert at all times, especially in bad weather. I never know when I will need one of them or all of them to do what is essential. When I do need them I need them with their full faculties and now.

I like navigating. I got into sailing because I was a humanities student at the University of Havana and Fidel came to our college. He lectured about taking up practical work to advance the revolution. He mentioned that the country needed maritime officers. I had an opportunity to speak with Fidel. Well, I enrolled as a deckhand apprentice on one of the first ships that Cuba bought. It was the East German-made Sierra Maestra. I was in the first graduating class for captains after the revolution. Besides me there was your friend Urquiola and Ramon Pérez. We were the Revolution's first three captains. My first captaincy was on that Sierra Maestra. Later, she became the first of our ships to be pensioned. And when we bought these Chinese ships, we used Sierra Maestra again for what is now our Giorita. Sixty transoceanic voyages during two decades of long distance sailing has it been so far. There is always diversity, always new challenges and new faces. You remember each trip for some reason, some event, some person. I love to learn and a sailor's life is filled with new learning challenges. I'm learning French now, for example, through the use of computer programs.

Contributing to the economy, doing a good job, gives me plenty of satisfaction. And there are many compensations, more so than negative aspects to sailing. The job, however, is a risky one. It may seem tranquil now but the sea is unpredictable and perilous. We don't think much about it but we put our lives in nature's hands. I've never experienced the necessity of abandoning ship or a foundered ship, but not long ago one of the most frightful events during my career occurred when we lost seven containers due to bad weather in Europe. We could have foundered that time.

Being away from my family so much and so long is the main deficit. We are also out of contact with much of our society's realities. For instance, we have a tough time now understanding the hardships of daily life under the current special period. The situation is very difficult now. Our country confronts the same pressures that all Latin societies do PLUS we must combat the pressures of the United States blockade. Otherwise, we have the same problems: depressed world prices for our raw materials and agricultural produces, high prices for those products we must import, an unpayable, ever-growing debt. But we have advantages that no other Latin or Third World country has. What we do have is distributed evenly—basically—instead of concentrated in the hands of a few. Our social structure is stable and the entire population receives a livable social security. All this provides us with a sense of tranquility.

When we have blackouts because of lack of petroleum everyone is effected equally. But in the Dominican Republic, just to take an example, only the poor are affected by blackouts. The rich are exempted from such inconveniences. The rich have their own generators. The rich have the best education, and in some places only the rich receive education. Only the rich are assured decent medical care in much of the world. The West considers all this inequality, all this suffering amongst the poor as necessary for "democracy": the logic of the free market economy.

Why are there epidemic diseases throughout the Third World, even in the US, and yet not in Cuba? Havana is one of the filthiest cities in the world yet there are no epidemics. The reason lies in socialism: our food and water are clean because we have a solid infrastructure and because we employ scientists and technicians to constantly check health conditions. We maintain hygienic infrastructures, and enforce rules against selling foods and drinks on the streets, which so easily can become contaminated. Even under special period there is no real hunger nor do the health and education systems crumble as they do elsewhere. Psychologically, some of our people feel hungry, because they were used to eating as much as they wished when Comecon existed.

Our main battle today is to survive, to struggle against every pressure threatening our socialism and independence. That is not to say that we haven't committed, and continue to commit, many stupidities.

One of our problems is that we feel isolated and as such we magnify our problems. We are geographically an isolated island without easy direct communication with other peoples. Only those with money can visit us and our people cannot readily visit other lands. It is principally a geographic and economic problem. Because of this, Cubans see their problems as bigger than they are and they complain and complain.

The objective limitations concerning communication and information are compounded by the political criteria for what is proper information and news to divulge. We lack internal information. I would like to know, for instance, why we don't have more energy sources, such as alcohol made from sugar cane like they do in Brazil. Why can't I get such information in Cuba? I simply don't know where to go to get answers.

News is viewed in two ways: what happens in capitalist countries is ipso facto negative; what happens in socialism is positive. News is not a question of reporting what is seen or experienced but is interpreted as `negative' and `positive'. `Positive', of course, is that which aids the battle to survive. I can understand the motivation but the results are often too simplistic.

We are educated people...on the one hand. Yet people are not educated, on the other hand, to know what an effective economy entails. We haven't learned how to confront the complicated problems of creating an effective economy. We have broken the monopoly of private property and put property in social terms, but who is conscious of being the social owner, the responsible one? Socialism is a grand society for all but we haven't realized individual responsibility in practice. As a consequence, many workers don't feel obligated to work well. They don't identify as the creators, beneficiaries and owners.

How do you educate properly? Periodic propaganda campaigns are disseminated through television, on posters and billboards, and in the schools. But Latinos are not routinized, consistent people. Our culture resists controlling mechanisms. Cultural traits are not easy to change or eradicate. Cubans like spontaneity and adventure. Consistency is boring. Fidel is also Cuban. He makes mistakes too because of these cultural traits. But he is different than most because he sees and admits his mistakes. It is worth the price to pay for his mistakes because his virtues are greater.

Another problem is work place democracy. Cuban workers have more impute in decision-making than under capitalism. The mass organizations have much to say about government matters, but in work centers there is a great lack of participation, although still more than under capitalism. Lack of participation in economic planning results in poor quality production and is part of the reason why workers don't feel like owners. Yet workers themselves lack consciousness to demand more say.

The major problem in the maritime industry is the lack of spare parts, delayed repairs, and insufficient petroleum. I don't honestly know if there are sufficient funds to buy what is necessary, but the reality is we run on far fewer legs than we could and than we need. I think the problem could be solved with the same money and resources by using intelligent, effective coordination. Our socialism is often too inflexible. We don't design systems and methods, products and packaging in the best ways. We don't present our products and services in attractive and comfortable ways as is done in capitalism. This affects people's self-image. They prefer products and services they see in capitalism.

These are problems we must tackle, and attempts to reform in some areas are being made. We are on a far better path than any other Third World Country. Cuba will come out of its crisis. There is no other choice. I'm convinced the future of humanity depends on adopting communism as its goal. It looks like it will be later than hoped for, later than should have been possible. I'm no ideologue but I've been a Communist all my life and will continue to be. Personally, I don't want to think about what Cuba will look like nor what will happen once Fidel dies. I don't want to outlive Fidel. Let him be where he is."

The 10th of October is commemorated for Manuel de Céspedes' 1868 declaration of independence from Spain. Céspedes was an attorney and small plantation owner in Camagüey province. He freed his 50 slaves in 1868, and together they initiated the Ten Years War of independence. Although victory escaped the Mambisa guerrilla army, it set the stage for the liberation war led, in 1896, by poet José Martí, who was killed in battle shortly thereafter. This liberation war resulted in victory over Spain but not before the United States found an excuse to intervene—sinking of the battleship Maine—as the liberationists were nearly defeating the Spanish. The US forced the Cuban victors to accept United States military superiority, which included seizing part of Guantánamo province for both its nickel reserves and a large area for the naval base it then built and claimed in perpetuity.

On this day, Giorita's Communist party nucleus and the seamen's union decided to hold an assembly to announce and discuss the voyage's goals and general conditions.

The youngest seaman aboard ship, Eduardo, 27, who was an officer candidate, read a commemorative historical sketch of Céspedes and the 10th of October declaration. The meeting was conducted by the union steward, the party leader and the cook, who called upon the captain to make opening remarks.

"This is a normal trip yet with little to export, an indication of the severe economic times we live. I don't know what we will be carrying back. On our last trip, we had $2000 to buy a few spare parts. This time we have no funds. This means we must be all the more careful with what we have; we must protect our ship all the more: no negligence, no waste, no breakage. We must close the doors behind us and not allow them to bang—not only because of the noise but to keep them from falling off the hinges. We have no more hinges.

"Sometimes I feel more like a kindergarten teacher than a ship's captain. This is your home. You spend more time here than in your family home. Treat it as you would want to be treated."

The chief engineer then explained that the liners were in good order and that the Japanese company would soon replace all of them. Modesto was concerned about the fuel they had loaded in Havana, a mixture of national crude oil and imported diesel. He said that other ships using this cheap mixture had experienced problems with their engines.

Each department head gave a report of their section. The main message was "preserve".

The captain spoke again after it was announced that there were no more light bulbs for cabins and general living quarters.

"I'm told there is thievery of light bulbs and even toilet seats. I'm told it isn't our men but stevedores. Even if that is so, why can't we watch out for our own ship? You men could prevent thievery, goddamnit. If thievery isn't stopped, if negligence isn't stopped, this ship will become a junk yard like so many others we've seen and then you'll be out of a job."

The party secretary took up the theme.

"Port authorities told me in Havana that they are now making regular checks to see that officers of the day actually maintain their posts and are vigilant. Seven ships have been fined for watch negligence. A pilot's launch and tug boat were nearly stolen in recent weeks."

The men did not raise anything to discuss so the meeting ended. The purser set four bottles of Caney rum on the table with ice and limes. The cook passed around trays of sausages, a taco concoction and olives. As we drank the excellent rum, I talked about its previous owners, the family Bacardi. They fled the revolution and became key financial backers to sabotage actions against Cuba. Not only are they criminals against all international laws, even US laws, which, on paper, respect all nation's sovereignty. Bacardi also produce such shitty quality rum now—not at all the original recipe, which the rebellious workers had and they continued making that rum under the new brand name—that they never advertise to drink it straight but together with their brother-in-international-crime, Coca Cola. There were cheers and toasts. We consumed everything in an hour.

I couldn't sleep for the rattles and creaks, the heaving, so I went to the bridge and kept Raúl company. I asked him why there was so much noise.

"It's the swells," he said. "There is always swelling in the deep and we're in waters of between 4000 and 5000 meters with winter winds, so the swells are greater. They come from the bottom of the sea and are aggravated by winds, tides, currents—all provoked by the moon. Think of a swell like a glass of water, which you stir with your fingers. When you take your fingers out of the glass, the entire body of water is whirling about. Swells can extend across the entire ocean. And because our ship is carrying a light cargo we feel the long rolling waves all the more. It'll be like this for the rest of the voyage, so just get used to it, Ron."

We had to hold on to something solid from time to time. The vessel tilted between 15 and 25 degrees. The climometer goes up to 55 degrees. "Beyond that we get into trouble," Raúl said, matter-of-factly. "I once experienced a listing of 80 degrees. I held my breath for a long long minute before she came to again."

I passed the captain's cabin on my way to bed. He was up and his door open.

"Come on in, Ron. I'm working out a program for balancing the ship during swells. You see," he explained gleefully, "a short vessel has a tendency to ride up one side of a wave and down the other side. Larger vessels can cut through a wave on an even keel. But if the wave is of such a length that the bow and stern are alternatively in successive crests and troughs, the vessel suffers sag and hog stresses. Under extreme conditions the ship can break in two.

"A wave considerably longer than the vessel can place the ship in danger of falling off into the trough. A cresting wave can be higher than a swell during storms. Swells do not crest sharply and are of greater force. They are like electronic oscillations, making longer and broader motions. If successive waves strike the side of a vessel at the same place as successive rolls, relatively small waves can cause heavy rolling and pitching. To reduce this one's heading and speed must be changed. I'm tracing on the computer the friction created by bending, shearing and torsion, which creates the creaking cries that keep you awake. I'm attempting to improve our programs to learn more precisely the degree of these various motions so that we can take preventive maneuvers."

I retired to my bunk, my little head totally confused. It was the first night that I felt chilly and had to use a blanket. Instead of passing urine once a night, my normal bladder demand, I had to pee half a dozen times. After a restless night, I spoke with Galinda about this.

"It's normal. Nobody is sleeping well just now. The chilly weather, the change of time zones, and the swells bother everybody. I didn't sleep well last night either. This is part of being a sailor."

I swayed to the bow stem and bent over as the bulb sprang out of the surface and then fell down spraying foam like a whale. Two-meter high waves smacked the hull causing the bulb to bob while plunging ever forward. No sailors were on deck so I scurried back, not wanting to irritate the captain for being alone on deck. I showered holding onto a handle bar with my back pressed into a corner so I wouldn't slip. I dried off with one hand and lay down so I wouldn't be knocked down. The next few days brought more of the same and I gradually got used to it.

I awoke to a calm day, the first in many. We had passed far south of the Azores and were nearing the Mediterranean. I took a tour of the ship ending at the bow stem. I watched low rippling swells. I had no sense of time. The ocean's omnipresent, undulating motion drew me magnetically. I saw nothing but blue blue blue. I heard nothing but the incessant, beckoning SWOOSH. Mesmerized, I desired to join her loins. I caught myself leaning half-way over the gunwale. Am I ready to plunge? It would be so easy, Ron. This woman, however, would not return me once coupled. She would conceal me forever in her womb. I backed off.

Near Disaster in the Mediterranean

Helmsmen were now at the wheel watching for increased traffic as we neared the Canary Islands. In the open sea with little traffic, bridge watch was conducted only by the officer on duty.

We'd been at sea for more than two weeks when I called Grethe ship-to-shore to wish her happy birthday. Then a voice over the VHF broke through:

"This is US Navy warship 06 to merchant ship 400 yards off your starboard bow, over."

Through binoculars we could see two aircraft carriers and a cruiser. Then a faint shoreline came into vision. It was the north coast of Morocco, the first land we'd seen in ten days. Traffic thickened and the captain took over the bridge. He commanded the helmsman to change direction periodically as small fishing craft popped up around us. The wheelhouse doors were shut to keep out the cold. Fog clouded the sea. The captain sounded the fog horn. We veered sharply to our port side to avoid a small fishing boat.

"Goddamn fishermen!" exclaimed Captain García, his jowls tight.

"They don't think about the big ships. They only think about the fish. It's always like this coming into the straits. Now I have to earn my money," he chuckled.

The captain walked rapidly from one side of the bridge to the other, binoculars up to his eyes, shouting new courses to the helmsman. Flag-masted blue buoys bobbed all around us as we entered the large-mouth Strait of Gibraltar. We could now see both Spain and Morocco coasts.

"What the hell! Are you at 0 8 5 degrees?" Captain García roared suddenly and rushed to the helm. He looked at the dial as he seized the wheel and swerved it port side. "BACK OFF!" he yelled at the helmsman.

The helmsman stepped back two strides and silently watched wide-eyed as the ship barely missed a tiny boat nearly under its starboard bow. The captain gripped the helm with one hand. He held binoculars to his eyes with the other. Half a dozen men and Galinda stood on the bridge breathless. We watched the captain and the sea in deep silence.

When we were out of danger, the helmsman spoke softly.

"I can take over now, Captain."

"No. I'll steer. You go home," he replied firmly.

The helmsman retreated from the wheelhouse.

The captain maneuvered the helm with his eyes glued to the binoculars. He called over the intercom for the first mate to present himself. Within seconds the first mate walked into the bridge. Another helmsman followed, as if in anticipation.

"That fellow is finished. Tell him to report for deck duty exclusively," Captain García told the first mate, agitatedly.

"Certainly, captain. What happened?"

"That idiot turned the ship to 150 degrees when I told him 0 8 5. He didn't repeat the new course. He had the ship headed in the wrong direction. I had to take over and watch the sea and a fishing boat at the same time. He's crazy. He's finished."

"Yes captain. You know, he was a politico before. This was his first time at the helm in years," explained the first mate.

"Politico! That explains it," the captain said, flatly.

The new helmsman relieved the captain and he walked out the port door with binoculars in hand as a large container ship passed in front of our bow several hundreds meters away.

"What a wonderful ship! I'd love to navigate her," the captain said to no one in particular, the harrowing experience now behind him.

I grabbed a pair of binoculars. It was a big Danish ship of the Mærsk line, owned by Denmark's richest capitalist, A. P. Møller. The "legitimized" war criminal made billions transporting oil, war equipment, even soldiers for whatever war or "national conflict" the United States paid him for. He would do the same for his government when it later became a warring ally of the U.S.

The demoted helmsman returned to the bridge and stood quietly beside his relief. He stared at the sea and the helm for three hours, which would have been the remainder of his tour of duty.

We were well inside the 15-mile-long Strait of Gibraltar, eight miles wide at is narrowest and 23 miles at its widest. There were fishermen all about. They waved at us cheerfully. The captain leaned over the rail and cussed out loud.

At chowtime, I ventured to question the captain about the incident on the bridge. What would happen to the helmsman?

"Nothing. Nothing at all. He'll work on the deck. That's it."

"Can he ask for a committee hearing when he returns? Can he become a helmsman again?"

"He can do what he damn well pleases," replied the captain bluntly. "He could appeal. But one thing is crystal clear: He'll never steer the helm of any ship I captain. You have to understand. I nearly became disoriented. After I gave orders to swing to 0 8 5 degrees—and I didn't say, as I never do, 085. No, I spell out course directions: ZERO EIGHT FIVE DEGREES. All of a sudden, I didn't know where I was. When you're lost with traffic around you that is deadly! You don't get a second chance to make a mistake like that, one that could kill human beings, and bring international ridicule to the ship, the captain, even the nation."

The tension of the close call, and the novelty of seeing land and fishing boats, kept me awake much of the night. It was also difficult to sleep because I had become accustomed to the rolling rough sea and now it felt like we were on a glassy mountain lake. But the Mediterranean is still a deep body of water: 2000 meters is common but its greatest depth is 4,700 meters. It is larger than the Caribbean: 1,145,000 square miles compared to 750,000. But it is similar in temperature and is likewise surrounded by many lands. On the north is Spain, France, Italy, Yugoslavia, Albania, Greece and Turkey. On the south is Morocco, Algeria, Tunis, Libya and Egypt. It culminates in the east at Syria and Jordan. And the Mediterranean encompasses many islands: Balearic, Corsica, Sardinia, Sicily, Crete and Cyprus.

Although it was now calm, the Mediterranean has fooled many. It is filled with ships sunken by the fury of winds and powerful waves, especially around the Balearic tourist islands.

Social life aboard ship changed radically once we came within range of television reception. The men ceased playing dominos, stopped watching their worn-out video films, and listening to Cuban music. They even chatted less. Their attention was now focused on television. They watched everything and seemed most eager for the advertisements, non-existent in state-supported Cuban television. News programs were totally different than in Cuba and, as such, were an object of interest as well. Even the captain and his partners ceased playing video games and cards to watch television. He never found time to play chess.

I had set my alarm clock for 0330 so I could experience our approach to Barcelona. The captain was on the bridge when I entered. We were earlier than initially plotted. A change in course had allowed us to miss a minor storm. Captain García called the pilot office. A pilot would board three miles out from harbor. The ship didn't have to heave to; it just slowed down enough to pick up the pilot from his launch.

"Pilots in Barcelona, just like the stevedores, are on time," the captain said, quite pleased.

Our ETA (estimated time of arrival) had been 14 days, 15 hours. We made it with three hours to spare.

Barcelona harbor is long and narrow. Tall cranes filled the skyline like locusts. The pilot, a man of similar age and build as Captain García, called out direction changes while leaning over a railing. Our captain liked to be involved so he repeated the course headings to the first mate, who, in turn, repeated them to the helmsman.

At 0630, two tug boats pushed us into a container pier and by 0645 we were smoothly moored at berth 18. I looked upwards from the bridge to the control cabin of a gigantic crane, much bigger than those in Cuba. An operator sat inside ready to maneuver the six-story tall monster. It took only a few minutes before our deckhands fixed the gangway and the civil guard and consignatory people boarded. An officer looked over our passports and handed them back to the purser. Everything was in order. The consignatory representative took the purser's cargo papers, check them, and handed them to the officer. No customs officials had come, as was routine in Cuba. Within half an hour, the paperwork was deemed in order and unloading began at 0825. They were to unload 210 empty containers and 12 partially filled ones. Three trucks lined up beneath the crane ready to drive off with two containers each. The captain shook the Spaniards hands and they departed. He turned to me with a big smile.

"You see, Ron, it is possible to be efficient. We made it on time. They were on time. We started unloading rapidly." The captain was pleased.

I was ready to ride my bicycle to the city. Galinda and the first headed me off at the gangway.

"Ron, you must be careful," Galinda said, seriously. "You don't know the city. You could get into trouble on the bicycle."

"You see the cemetery up ahead, across the motorway?" the first mate asked. "Well, there are a lot of gypsies that live or hang out around that cemetery. When strangers come by they often jump them and steal whatever they have. Your bicycle is a good target. Then the motorway itself is very busy and drivers aren't careful about cyclists. If you do manage to get by the cemetery and through the motorway, you're likely to meet groups of AIDS-infected people in town. Some of them have been known to carry syringes with their infected blood and jab people with them out of anger and spite. They want to get more attention about their plight, hoping the government will do something to help them. Many people are desperate here, Ron. You have to be careful. I recommend that you don't ride your bicycle. Take a bus or taxi into town."

I was overwhelmed by their concern. I didn't feel the same sense of danger but still I consented to leave my bike behind. Cuban people are so caring I didn't want to disappoint them, nor did I want them to change their caring ways. I spotted a taxi and the chauffeur left me at the entrance of the famous, picturesque Rampla. I hadn't seen any gypsies or AIDS terrorists. Nevertheless, I was surprised by what I did see. I hadn't been out of Cuba in three years and never in Barcelona. It didn't seem so "Spanish" to me. Just another European commercialized city: businesses, bars and restaurants jammed on top of or next to one another. Consumer goods galore. Everything prettily packaged. Staggering prices. Street musicians and performers did their bit for loose change in and around many kiosks. While they were stacked with scores of periodicals, I didn't see any left-wing publications. Vendors said they had none or that the media was "no longer politically oriented". That was hard to believe. At the eighth kiosk, I asked if he had a left-oriented publication.

"What is that?" a bewildered vendor asked.

I gave up.

Except for an occasional beggar, people were rushing about like they had important appointments. Many were well dressed and wore wrist watches they glanced at compulsively. A man in front of a foreign currency exchange business was trying to entice by-passers with the infamous slight-of-hand trick. I found a store with typewriter ribbons, a rarity, and bought a "Brother" ribbon for my portable model. The rest of my time in Barcelona was spent at bar counters, drinking tasty dark beer. I spent more money in the eight hours in Barcelona than I usually did in Cuba in eight weeks, and I had nothing but a typewriter ribbon and satisfied taste buds to show for it. I found a handful of seamen heading back to Giorita on their bicycles—they had not been warned, obviously. One gave me a lift.

At 1800, we were all aboard ship as ordered. The containers had been unloaded and the remainder relatched. We sailed at 2000. In the 12 hours at Barcelona port, the stevedores had accomplished in one normal shift what had taken the Cienfuegos stevedores more than three days to do. But the difference wasn't due to "Latin laziness" as much as it was to the blockade, to the fact that Cuba was being daily sabotaged in many ways and Spain was not. This reality was not always a part of our consciousnesses, not even those of us who lived and worked in solidarity with Cuba, and not even for all Cubans. Still, one could wonder if inefficiency is synonymous with Cuban socialist social security, with the affectionate, fun-loving people, while capitalist efficiency is synonymous with nervous insecurity and aloofness.

Silence on the Bridge

We passed the next 36 hours uneventfully. We should dock at Amsterdam at noontime on the 26th of October. Early morning on the 22nd, we sighted Gibraltar again. Since all was going smoothly, I could watching this narrow rocky promontory four kilometers long pass by. It is one of Britain's few crown colonies left. The mountain island, with its classic fortress, is a strategic location between Morocco and Spain and has been ruled by one or the other many times. It was used during World War 11 as a springboard for the Anglo-American invasion of North Africa. Today, Gibraltars's 30,000 inhabitants earn comfortable livelihoods off tourism, fishing, and the fueling and repair station for naval and merchant ships.

As we neared the strait's mouth, we heard a loud explosion and a cloud rose from the sea ahead. The captain radioed the Tarifa station. "It's just a routine firing practice in the submarine exercise zone; nothing to worry about." Nevertheless, the spell of tranquility was broken.

We were soon in the Atlantic heading northwest towards the coast of Portugal. The sea turned choppy as we sailed straight into the wind and our speed dropped to 11 knots. Eduardo was at the helm. He had graduated from the naval academy and was finishing his in-service training. Before this assignment he had been with the Shark.

"I prefer this ship over the tankers," he told me. "Long distance cargo voyages are more comfortable. There is more space. And this container, like most cargoes, is in better condition. Even newer tankers get worn out fast. What I did like about the cabotaje was seeing parts of my country I'd never seen before. I can't complain about any of the ships and voyages I've taken. I've seen and learned so much. I feel lucky."

Figure 13: Giorita Captain Carlos García spying Gibraltar, 1992.

"Dolphins! Ron, look, dolphins at the bow," yelled Eduardo's relief, as he came onto the bridge.

Small dolphins were jumping up playfully off the port bow. The crew knew I'd been looking for dolphins the entire trip. I had felt friendly with these water mammals ever since I'd played with them in Brazil's Atlantic just a stone's throw from where I lived. These were the first I'd seen on this trip. I rushed to my cabin for my camera and half ran to the bow. The sea hit the hull a bit roughly but it didn't phase me. I leaned over the bow stem and saw a dozen cute dolphins twisting around as they swam abreast, showing off. Some were grayish brown, others were black with white underbellies. They were smaller than those I knew in Brazil. They swam uniformly, crossing from port to starboard and back over, jumping up and away from the bulb before its nose plunged downward. They splashed about like children.

I snapped photo after photo oblivious to anything else. I swung my left leg over the railing and raised my body up slightly so I could better see the creatures and click the camera. When I finished the roll of film, I brought my leg to the deck and glanced back at the bridge far away. I could make out blurry figures looking at me from behind the large windshield. I'd better return, I thought. When I reached the bridge, I caught sight of the captain's back as he descended the interior staircase. There was an unusual stillness on the bridge. The helmsman spoke softly without looking at me.

"The captain wishes to see you in his cabin."

When I arrived at the captain's cabin his door was shut. I knocked and entered when told to. Captain García spoke immediately.

"What were you doing on deck?"

"I was photographing dolphins."

"Did you see any seamen on deck?"

"No sir."

"No, you didn't, and you won't for a long time. We're coming into a storm. Couldn't you see the swells rising? Are you not clear about the fact that any wave at any time could have knocked you over the railing? You would have drowned with no possibility of rescue. I could have been jailed for your irresponsibility, dammit!"

"I am sorry sir. I'm sorry I upset you. I wasn't thinking..."

"Se ronca el mango (3). I can't risk any mishap aboard ship. You are restricted to the interior for the rest of the voyage. That is all."

I shut my door and drew the curtains to the port holes and crawled in bed. I felt like a spanked child who knows he fucked up. I had broken a key safety rule, one that could have cost me my life. And I had let Captain García down. He had treated me so kindly and fairly. I respected him so, as did all the men. I felt ashamed.

I spent the rest of the day and night in bed. I awoke the next morning to the sound of rain. I went to the bridge. The captain greeted me normally. I asked for forgiveness and he said, "Forget it. I have. Look at the weather instrument, Ron. It shows the winds are blowing at 26 knots. A storm is approaching from the north. We've slowed down to ten knots."

The captain changed course and revised our ETA by 24 hours. He stayed on the bridge, except for a quick nap now and then, for three days until the storm left us.

I went down to the mess hall for coffee and a roll. No one looked at me as an outcast. I was still an all right person.

I went to my cabin to write. The ship rocked throughout the day, knocking objects off the table. I was typing one instant and on the floor the next holding my typewriter on my lap. The chair flew into the port wall. Everything on the desk was on the floor. The jolt could easily have occurred yesterday when I was on deck, I thought.

I gradually made my way to the bridge, holding onto railings and walls as I stumbled forward. The climometer was jiggling from 25 to 35 degrees. Swells surged spraying into creamy crescendo curls and then falling into abyssal troughs.

"Welcome to the Bay of Biscay," Captain García shouted at me over the storm's roar, "the black hell."

We were passing Cabo Finisterre and entering the large bay that is so often tempestuous. Seamen refer to seasickness as "Biscay dizziness", because storm conditions are so common here. Northern and southern European seas meet here. The Mediterranean is not far to the south and the English Channel is to the north. The route between Cabo Finisterre and Ile d'Ouessant, the southern France entrance to the English Channel, is 377 miles by chart and should have taken 27 hours to cross. But we had to make many direction changes as the winds and waves sometimes stopped our forward motion altogether. We were often heading due east, then suddenly northeast, then northwest and even due west—zig zagging across the gulf. We were in a gale force 8 for most of three days and two nights. Winds blew at between 30 and 40 knots and waves swelled between four and six meters. Our ship once listed 42 degrees. We were continuously being jostled. It wasn't possible to sleep more than a few minutes or an hour or two at a time.

Silence permeated the bridge. The helm was never set on automatic. Either the captain or the officer on duty or the helmsman steered with hands clamped on the wheel. Waves would sometimes smack directly at the bow or stern and lap over gunwales onto the main deck. The captain struggled to turn the helm, in order to avoid direct hits. The sea rolled and broke into spindrifts hour after hour. Foam blew in streaks everywhere one could see. Visibility was often no more than a few dozen meters. We could rarely stand up without holding onto a solid structure. Crewmen were knocked about and everything not bolted down lay on the floor. My coffee table top had been yanked out of its screws and thrown against a wall. The captain's office was a mess with file folders all over the floor.

"I want to be in port. I am tired of this sea," the doctor told me on the second day. "I can't sleep. The captain never rests more than a short nap. Look at his face, Ron. It is swollen with allergic reaction."

The captain stood by the radar. His cheeks were red and puffed out.

The skies were so overcast and filled with spray that we would not have seen another ship if it was too close to us. It was necessary to study the screen in order to determine if there were ships nearby.

I asked Captain García what he thought about during the storm.

"I think only of my job: of avoiding being broken up by the sea, of avoiding collisions with vessels, of avoiding the worst of weather. This time it wasn't possible," he laughed. "But this is a noble gale, not as bad as most cyclones. It is more uncomfortable than dangerous. It is all the more uncomfortable because the ship isn't carrying its full weight. What is most risky is if we dip into a trough at the same time we are broadsided. Containers could come unlatched and topple. That would founder us."

He fell silent. Only the surge of the sea slapping at the hull could be heard.

"I feel fear too. It would be a lie to say I didn't," he added a minute later.

Captain García had been in enough bad weather to have the sense to be afraid, though it did not incapacitate him. I, on the other hand, was experiencing my first real gale. I was exhilarated more than frightened. It was an adventure, and I was an observer removed from the requirements of responsibility. I was glad I was not in an aircraft in storm weather where I'd be totally helpless. But on this ship, I could see what the "pilot" was doing. I could hang onto the ship or a lifeboat, or perhaps swim. Suddenly, my romantic thoughts switched to rationality. If the sea was so wrathful that it could break up a ship, it would certainly consume me as well. Although I was deluding myself about possibilities of surviving a toppled ship, I felt safe. I think Captain García pertinacity and skills had a lot to do with that feeling.

As the hours turned into days, my joints stiffened from planting my legs and feet so firmly on the ground. My limbs grew tense and tired. My flesh was bruised in several places from being knocked against cabinets and walls. We had to eat holding our plates. The table cloths were soaked with spilled liquid. It wasn't possible to take a shower. One had to sit on the toilet to urinate. We all let our whiskers grow. I couldn't write anymore. I spent most of my time on the bridge fascinated by the maneuvers, the silent tension. Sometimes I'd read. When I finished the book on Colombus, I found some articles about "Orion", a hero of mine.

"Orion" was the Cuban State Security counterintelligence code name for José Ramón Fernández Brenes. He was the television director-writer-editor who had infiltrated the U.S.'s propaganda television station, TV-Martí. Brenes had faked his loyalty for United States "democracy" by "escaping from Communist Cuba". In the spring of 1988, Brenes received permission as a television director to board a Cuban merchant ship in Havana. He was to make a television novel about Cuban seamanship. The night before the freighter docked in Canada, the captain told Brenes:

"You know, chico, nobody has ever stayed behind on me."

The next day, Brenes left the ship and made his way to New York where he met with a Cuban agent handler. Posing as a refugee, he soon acquired interviews with Radio Martí directors in Washington. In May 1985, the US launched Radio Free Cuba, nicknamed Radio Martí after Cuba's legendary liberator from Spanish colonialism. Ironically, José Martí was a severe critic of US expansionism. In a May 1896 letter to a friend, Martí had written: "I have lived in the monster, and I know its entrails; my slingshot is that of David."

Brenes had impressed the radio directors, who were preparing for the television equivalent of Radio Martí, with his resume of 25 years working in all phases of Cuban television programming. Having planted seeds, he settled in Miami. A year later, he was contacted to work with the $32 million television subversion project to sow discord inside Cuba.

Reading about "Orion", I recalled the privilege I had of witnessing TV Martí's first day of broadcasting. I was one of the international and national journalists invited by Communications Minister Manuel Castillo Rebassa to attend Cuba's jamming operation. We had arrived at the tall communications building at 0300. The minister explained that within minutes the US would be illegally sending a program from a satellite in Miami over a balloon above the Florida Keys, which in turn would transmit to Cuba. A high-powered antenna on top of the building would intercept its transmission and then technicians would jam it. The minister asked for a journalist volunteer to give the order to jam. I was one who raised a hand and he called on me. I was honored to give the jamming order, making a blow against the imperialist nation in which I was born. I asked for Nicaragua's Sandinista reporter to accompany me. I stood and placed my finger next to an intercom. The minister stood close by before a wide blackboard under a logo—Teleagresión—and beside it a large television set.

At 0345, TV Martí's director of programming, Alberto Roldán, appeared upon the television set. He came in quite clearly in full color. "Good morning Cuba. This is Tele Marti." Two journalists sat beside Roldán ready to introduce a world news report. Roldán started to read a text, which Cuban agent "Orion" had prepared.

"Mensaje especial para todos los cubanos. Queremos anunciarles que en este mismo momento sale al aire TV..." (4)

Minister Castillo nodded and I pushed the intercom button. In a deep, excited voice I said: "Interfere! Dale!" (5)

The picture disintegrated. And so has it been ever since that day. The US sends the signal three hours a day at the cost of many millions of dollars, which the congress appropriates each year. And Cuba jams it. Sometimes it needs to deploy air and naval units to help plug gaps in its stationary electronic intervention. But no one sees the "Invisible Television", as many locals call it. Many governments have complained to the UN that the US violates the International Telecommunications Convention, which both the US and Cuba signed. The Convention prohibits any nation from interfering with another's "sovereign right to regulate its telecommunications". The US tried to send its signal over one of Cuba's dozen TV channels, Tele Rebelde on Channel 13. The US counters that it is defending "freedom", as President George Bush told US broadcasters a week after the Department of State, in cooperation with General Electric, began sending its program (6). Many of these broadcast executives criticized TV Martí, because of its illegality and because Cubans had, as they stated, access to outside information. Some Cubans listen to one of several normal radio stations in the southern part of the US, as Cuban officials pointed out. They added that Cubans enjoy watching US films sent by Cuban television. The previous year, for instance, Cubans could see 288 US-made films broadcast on Cuban television.

Figure 14: Minister of Communications, Manuel Castillo Rebasa, explains to journalists in Havana that the U.S. television signal, TV Martí, as they call it and which Cubans call aggression TV (telegresión), is about to be launched that morning, March 25, 1990.

In something which must have been inspired by "Alice in Wonderland", the US administration accused Cuba of violating international laws (unnamed), because it jammed the illegal US transmissions. Furthermore, the US Federal Communications Commission complained to Cuba for sending a speech by Fidel Castro condemning US media aggression, which Americans could hear in some states.

It was my hero "Orion" who had supplied the Cuban government with information that allowed it to know in advance what the CIA-created television station was planning. His information helped technicians to jam the signal. "Orion" continued working for TV Martí for the next 15 months until he was called back to Havana.

I read these articles, thinking of the glorious moment I had in defying the empire's duplicity, while the gale roared on but with diminished capacity. By the third day, it had dropped to Force 5 and our speed increased to 14 knots. We were soon out of the storm but the ocean was still choppy and another gale warning was forecast further north. We came into sounding water—less than 1000 meter depth, shallow enough to be measured by sounding—and the waters calmed.

On October 26th, we sighted Ile d'Ouessant. The English Channel lay just ahead. We had sailed nearly twice the normal distance across the Bay of Biscay and in a period thrice normal. The sea was Force 4 and we breathed easy. In fact, it felt odd not to be swaying to and fro.

Captain García explained to me over dinner that although it is not obligatory, most ships choose to employ a pilot to guide them through the North Sea, the Skagerrak and Kattegat around Denmark, and through Øresund into the Baltic. A pilot knows best where the waters are too shallow and when warning markers have changed.

"Our ships always take on a pilot. We prefer the Dutch because they are the most knowledgeable and reliable. It may take 30 or more hours for a trip through these waters at a cost of two to three thousand dollars. But it is worth it," the captain said.

Shortly before midnight, we arrived outside Brixham and a pilot's launch drew alongside. The captain and I hung over the bridge railing to watch the pilot climb up the rope ladder. He slipped halfway up. A man below caught him and pushed him up the ladder. The third mate went to meet the pilot and he called the captain on a walky-talky.

"The pilot is coming and he is drunk."

"Ay, mi madre!" (7), the captain exclaimed.

A tall blond man dressed in navy blue sweater and sailor jacket wobbled onto the bridge. He greeted the captain with a big smile.

Captain García was in no mood for pleasantries.

"Are you ready to sail?" he asked the pilot.

"Yes."

"What course?" the captain asked, perfunctorily.

"094 degrees, full speed ahead."

The captain repeated the course to the helmsman and turned to the big man.

"OK, pilot, I'll take over now. You drink some coffee and the purser will take you to the infirmary where you can rest until morning."

"I'm here to help guide you. There's work going on in this part of the channel," the pilot slurred.

"That's all right. I'll manage. I'd rather that you rested and be fresh in the morning. Then I'll rest."

"Whatever you like, captain, but I can..."

"No problem. I'll take charge now," and the captain nodded to the purser to conduct him below.

When they'd gone, the captain shrugged and growled, "La puta que me parío." (8)

"I have no other alternative than to stay on the bridge all night. The pilot reeks of alcohol. The Dutch seamen have a prestigious reputation. If I reported him, he'd be sacked."

I watched the captain maneuver the ship around buoys and traffic for an hour and then I went to sleep. In the morning, a telex lay on the floor under my door: "Welcome to Amsterdam."

My friend from the Amsterdam Cuban solidarity committee had been contacted by Mambisa's consignatory office in Rotterdam and she would be waiting when we docked. How kind.

At mid-morning, we were sailing through the Strait of Dover, and soon we were in Belgium's part of the North Sea. The Dutch pilot had sobered up and was operating the passage. We entered the locks just after midnight. Amsterdam is below sea level, so to prevent flooding and to allow ships to pass into the harbor; locks were constructed to inhibit currents from over-swimming the harbor. Only one large ship can pass the narrow locks at a time. It took two hours to reach the container docks. We veered in at 0300, only 39 hours later than the original estimate from Barcelona. I saw Jose waving to me from the quay.

I shook hands around and gave an especially emotional one to Captain García.

At Jose's apartment, we toasted with a Havana Club and a Punch cigar she had saved for me.

A few days later, Mambisa's consignatory director in Rotterdam told me that the Giorita had unloaded and sailed to England where she underwent minor repairs. She was sailing over the Atlantic to Montreal when another storm in the Bay of Biscay rammed a Greek tanker, causing a spill of thousands of tons of oil. The storm also broke latches of a Philippine container crewed by Filipinos and Danes. Five Danish seamen were swept overboard with a bunch of containers in the same waters we had crossed a few days before.

Notes:

1. Runabout
2. Someone from Galicia, Spain, or someone with roots there.
3. The mango is sneezing—literally. An idiom meaning something absurd or incredible, or sarcastically: that is just great.
4. "This is a special message for all Cubans. We want to announce that at this very moment we are broadcasting on TV..."
5. Jam. Do it.
6. The idea for TV Martí came from the Ronald Reagan administration in 1987. Reagan first became a national name as the main TV advertising voice for General Electric.
7. "Oh, my mother!"
8. "The whore who was born to me."

Figure 15: Ron returns to Cuba on "Rose Islands", May 1993.

CHAPTER SEVEN: ROSE ISLANDS
Return to Cuba

"Coño! No me digas. Es Ron!" (1) I looked up from the dock and recognized Manso rushing down from the deck to embrace me.

That is one of the nicest aspects about sailing different ships: you meet former colleagues and work with them again. Unexpectedly being met by Manso as I came up to this new ship, which would take me back to Cuba, was a pleasant surprise. I had sailed with Manso on the Seaweed, a garrulous helmsman from Caibarién. Meeting his friendly face relieved some of the sadness I felt. I was once again leaving Grethe behind in Denmark.

I had been away from Cuba half-a-year, half of it living with Grethe in Copenhagen, and now it was time for me to return. She was against it but I had nothing of significance to do in Denmark. There was no revolutionary movement or socialism to fight for. Denmark was a placid land with a passive people, a nation all too tied—and gladly so—to the United States. Neither my politics nor my temperament was appreciated, and I had little enthusiasm for the tiny and impotent left. In Cuba, I was somebody because of my politics and temperament. Cuba was struggling to maintain its revolution and I identified with that. My work there could help spread solidarity so that it would make it all the more difficult for the United States to invade this thorn in its side. Grethe sometimes understood but did not accept my decision. She could not join me in this quest. We were often estranged from one another even when together. Yet we were so much drawn to each another in some inexplicable way that it was very painful to part. On May Day her brother drove me from Copenhagen to Rotterdam with my baggage. And now Manso was introducing me to the captain while my straw trunk was being placed on a pallet to be lifted aboard.

Captain Ramón Pérez Miranda was a tall handsome man. He was thin but well built. Graying around the temples, he carried himself in a quiet, self-assured manner. His big brown hands shook my small white hands firmly. The captain was interested that I had sailed with Manso and he invited me to his cabin for a longer talk. Once I spoke of my trip over on the Giorita, his calm face lit up.

"You sailed with Carlos García? Well, I'll be damn. We graduated together from the first captain's training course."

"Yes, Captain García told me that he and you, and Captain Urquiola, were the revolution's first captains. What a coincidence that I've sailed with you all! Coño!"

I was family from that moment on.

I didn't need to work but I asked to. I could decide on a daily basis where I wished to work or if I wished not to. I had paid for my passage. The captain introduced me to Jorge, the big-bellied chief engineer. Rose Islands was one of Cuba's largest container ships and the engine room was much bigger than I had seen. Rose Islands was much older than Giorita and there was grease everywhere, so I had work enough.

I had a fine cabin with port hole and desk. I brought my "Brother" typewriter to write up a report on my European and Southern California tours. But first I wanted to get acquainted and do a bit of physical work. I assisted half-a-dozen deckhands bring in the mooring lines and Rose

Islands sailed on time, albeit not with much cargo. We had no stops before Havana, which should take us three weeks to reach.

I sometimes sat with the officers at chow time, other times with the crew. Lazaro, the party secretary, and Luis, the union secretary, introduced me around. The crew was happy to be returning home after months away.

After our first dinner sailing, the woman stewardess introduced herself.

"I didn't hear where you are from but you aren't Cuban are you?"

"No."

"Are you Russian?"

"No."

"Czech?"

These were the two most frequent of a handful of earlier socialist states, which sometimes had a technician or more on Cuban ships.

"What are you then?"

"I am an internationalist," I proudly pronounced.

"Where is that?" she asked, perplexed.

Figure 16: "Rose Islands", Holland-Cuba, May 1993.

It was hot as hell but fun working in the engine room. Jorge was a jolly man and the men were happy to be with him. They spoke well of the captain, too, but he was not as out-going as their chief. When we were well out to sea and saw only blue, I decided to write up my report for the cultural ministry and who else in Cuba may be interested in what I had done during my travels. No one had asked me to report, but I wanted to show my "production" as a worker and activist for a valiant and equalitarian folk, and as compensation, so to speak, for the fact that I hadn't found a book publisher for the manuscript I had begun to write aboard the Giorita and finished in Copenhagen. I'd tried one in Denmark, which rejected it on the basis that there was too much praise for socialist Cuba and Fidel. Most of the dozen other publishers I sent it to in the United States and England thought the subject matter was interesting, the writing adequate enough, but the topic would not attract enough readers to make publication profitable. Most editors also thought it too problematic that I was a supporter of Cuba's socialism and thus communist ideology. The political climate in Europe, and of course in the United States, was against this. The fall of the Berlin Wall, the demise of the powerful Soviet Union and European Communist party governments had placed socialism in the waste paper basket, and publishers were not going out on the limb. I was downhearted about this and the probability that the manuscript would never get published. There was no hope in Cuba, not with the special period in full bloom.

It felt good, however, to summarize the sales of "Backfire", which I had sold to a few bookstores and during 40 talks. My tour began the day after the Giorita had docked in Amsterdam, then further to Germany and Denmark. In January, I traveled to many cities in England for a dozen talks then on to Southern California and northern Mexico. In all, I spoke to about 2000 people and was responsible for selling about 500 books. I had earlier sold 1,000 books in Cuba, having taken over the task of selling most of the 3,500 print run, because the Cuban publisher did almost nothing to distribute it, nor most of their other books. I earned a total of $10,000. Cuban institutions received $6000. My revenues paid for most of my traveling. I had also been interviewed by a score of print and radio media and wrote some articles.

We stopped suddenly in mid-Atlantic one bright warm day while I was painting the deck with half-a-dozen deckhands. Word came to us that the engine needed looking at again. We had stopped the day before to check it for a couple hours. Manso and a couple other men fetched spools of heavy line with large hooks fastened to an end.

"You want to fish, Ron?" Manso asked. "It looks like we might be stopped for a while. Here, take this spool and come with me."

We walked to the stern and dropped the hooks over the railing. The lines swished out. The men had a clever way of fastening the large spools between the railing and the strake. They should hold fast if a fish took a hook and ran with it. We left the spools to fish without us and returned to painting at mid-ship. In the course of the next hour or so, one or more of us went to stern every one in a while to check the lines. I went alone one time. The current kept the lines naturally stretched tight so it wasn't easy to see if we had any bites. I was standing at the stern over my spool when I saw IT. Something huge sprang out of the water a long way off. I couldn't believe my eyes. I grabbed for my spool. The line was very taut. I couldn't wind in even a centimeter. Then the beast sprang again and I could feel that we were connected. It was too far away to see what it was. Then I thought I could make out a large tail fin.

"SHARK. I've got a shark on the line! Help!" I yelled. My heart beat so hard I could hear it. I took the spool in both hands and just held on. I felt motion and line whirled out. I had no idea how I could bring in this monster with no rod or reel: just bare hands holding desperately onto this spool and hundreds of meters of line with one large hook attached to the end. I called out to the crew again as I brought the spool toward my chest and felt the beast tug.

"SHARK. Ron has a SHARK," one of the men yelled from behind me. Others came rushing to see this elongated vertebra "fish" jump from the ocean. The Thing was several meters long. The men were yelling at me to hold on, to wind in, to not drop the spool, to put on gloves...I just held on. On the next spring, I managed to grip the line and force one turn over the spool. When he dipped into the sea again there was a lapse and I managed to wrap line around twice. The monster was probably one meter closer to me. I felt pats on my back, a cheer and a coño. Then the shark dashed in a straight direction making the line taut again and burned my fingers. Now with both hands, I gripped the ends of the spool and brought it into my chest. Holding on.

The monster and I proceeded in this manner for some time: he dashing and darting underwater; me gripping the spool and holding it tightly into my chest. I could feel his surge upward, and then "reeling" in, one loop and then another. When he splashed down again, he was a few meters closer. But then he rushed so powerfully that line spun out from the spool. I grabbed the line with my right hand and it burned my palm again. I held onto the spool with both hands and raised it up and back toward my shoulders and then down into my chest. I gained a meter that way. So I made that motion again and it worked. Then the monster plowed outward and all I could do was hold on. When he surfaced the next time, I was ready for him and brought in a few turns of line. I felt only tension: tension in muscles, bones, tension in the men's voices, tension from the monster struggling for his life.

This was our rhythm now. He could stop my progress by holding out in one prolonged powerful plunge but when he veered or slacked, I wound in. I could sense that he was tiring; he was coming closer. I could make out a bluish tint to his body, and I shivered. This was MY SHARK! The Catch of a Lifetime!

In time, no sense of how long, his bluish body appeared just under the surface still long away but within eyesight. The shark was dodging as it approached. The crewmen were jabbering. Someone was saying, "How are we to bring him aboard deck?" Yeah, how? Someone produced a long hand harpoon. But how could that spear the shark from where we stood, so many meters above waterline? Another man came up with a long thick rope and he began making a lasso. I couldn't pay attention to their maneuvering. I had to hold on and wind line in whenever there was slack and now there was so much that I couldn't always keep up. Without a wheel handle, it was awkward "reeling" in fast enough. Although the shark fought on, I now had the advantage. I could make out one large eye and layers of long razor-sharp teeth. I noticed several men out of the corner of my left eye leaning over the port railing. One held the harpoon, another dangled the lassoed rope. The shark was so near now that I could decipher an eyelid drooping over an eye the size of my forehead. His body was broad and long, maybe four meters long and there were THREE layers of teeth. I wound in frantically. I must keep the line taut, fearing the hook could slip out. The shark was just before the bow and barely resisting. I wound the line in faster and faster. His immense body stilled beside the starboard hull. A seaman threw down the lasso by his tail and pulled it up again. I wound more line in. He threw the lasso again and it hit the finned tail. He slipped the lasso over the tail and heaved. Two men heaved with him. Now I could see my line leading into his gigantic mouth. HEAVE! They shouted. And the tail edged upward. But most of the body and head remained on the surface of the water. How can three or four men heave a several hundred kilo blue shark 20 or 30 meters up and over the gunwale with one rope attached only to its tail? There must be a second rope. But there was no time to find one. The rope slackened and the intelligent beast summoned its strength and launched forward. The men heaved again and I wound in a slack line. The tail slipped into the sea. I watched my catch, the catch of a lifetime, inch forward beside the bow. My heart sank. COÑO!

A hand clasped my shoulder from behind. My eyes remained glued to the blue shark returning to his blue Atlantic.

"Ron, you asked me yesterday when we stopped the engine if you could take a swim," Captain Pérez reminded me in a calm, slow voice. "I forbad you. You now have my permission to take your swim, if you still wish."

We were sailing again by chowtime. The topic of conversation was The Blue Shark and my struggle. The men were gay. Though they commiserated with my loss, they felt that the moment of struggle, the catch itself was the most significant aspect of the adventure. And not all had seen a blue shark, or such a large one. That was an eventful experience in itself. There was laughter, too, at the captain's dry humor. Someone said that blue sharks can live for 20 years and they have a memory, so it would be wise for me to keep out of the ocean.

The next day, another bright sunny day, the engine went on the blink again, the third time. Jorge was beside himself. The captain decided that rather than let the crew fish again, it would be more productive to test the two lifeboats. I watched as the starboard raft was lowered down empty. After it floated a few minutes, it was raised. The captain decided to test the portside lifeboat with human weight, thereby putting the pulley-wheel mechanism to a more realistic trial. There were to be two men at the bow and two at the stern. Naturally I wanted to participate. Captain Pérez gave me permission with strict instructions not to move from my seat. I was to help maintain balance and observe. We placed on life preservers and I sat behind a young officer. He would check the chain and hook connection at the bow. The first mate and a deckhand would do the same at the stern. The life-boat was held fast by chains from the pulley-wheel mechanism. At the end of each chain sat a large hook, which was clasped to a ring fixed at each end. As we were lowered slowly, the wheel mechanism proved to be a bit stubborn; it was difficult to maneuver evenly. Half way down, the raft tilted toward the bow. We were stopped in mid-air. The operator endeavored to straighten us and we were lowered again. But as we approached waterline we were again uneven. The bow lightly splashed into the sea as the stern was still above water, causing us to jerk. I heard the hook jiggle in the ring. I heard men high above us shouting but couldn't make out the words. Small but choppy waves splashed at the rubber life-raft's sides and we wobbled. The young third mate held onto the bow's unstable chain.

"The hook is loose!" shouted the first mate.

I looked at the stern to see a swinging chain. Now we were in real trouble. One end of the boat slapped against the ship while the other was pointed out towards the sea. The first mate tried to catch the chain while the deckhand tried to stabilize the craft with his hands. At the bow, the third mate was clearly nervous. I remained sitting, taking it all in. Both men at the stern were reaching for the wildly swinging hook and the boat was whirling in different directions. Suddenly a scream escaped from the first mate and he bent over and held one hand with the other. The hook had hit him. Shouts from above. The chain was swinging back and forth. It smacked into the hull and on its return over the life-boat, the deckhand managed to grasp it. He held on while he was reeling. He was too far from the ring to bring the hook to it. The first mate sat by the ring still holding his hand, his body rocking. A dangling rope caught my eye. A crew man was scrambling down the rope. He landed into the life-boat and took over for the first mate. He and the other man struggled with the chain and hook. At the bow, the third mate's eyes were bulging. The chain slipped from his hand. All the shaking and trembling caused the hook to come dislodged from the ring. More shouts. The boat was gyrating. We were totally unhinged from the ship.

I must act. I looked at the paralyzed third mate and stood halfway up and stepped forward and beside him. I had to hold onto a loop on top of the raft with my left hand, in order to prevent me from falling out. My baseball background reminded my eyes how to hold the swinging chain in sight, and told my right hand to snatch it as it came close to my nose. Just at that moment, I released my left hand from its grip and with both hands grasped the chain. The young officer did not budge. My body was now next to his as my hands slipped down the chain and hung onto the hook. I was swaying but maintained sufficient balance not to fall by holding fast. I waited no more than the necessary seconds until the swing of the boat brought the bow close to the hook and the ring was within reach. Now! I jabbed the hook into the ring and held fast with bare fingers. With the bow partially stabilized, the two men at stern managed to pull their hook into the ring. We had hooked the boat and the wavering diminished.

"HEAVE." I shouted. "Wheel in," we all shouted, except for the young officer, who was still paralyzed, and the first mate, who was shocked in agony. There was a jerking motion upward. Then the men at stern yelled that their chain was slack. The hook was not fastened tightly. More rocking again but it didn't get out of hand before they could fasten the hook adequately. Wheeling us up was a jerky, slow process. One end of the boat banged into the hull and the other swung out. Many men were winding us up over the wheel, which was not in good operating order. Hand heaving was uneven. The young officer had not changed expression and remained crumpled over. The first mate was wrinkled in pain. We jerked upwards bit by bit; bow up, then stern up. When we finally reached the railing, many hands lifted the first mate over and carried him to the medical clinic. Then the rest of us crawled out and stood on the lovely solid deck.

I looked at the men's faces as they received us. I was so glad to see no sign of contempt or degradation toward the young officer. They were not pleased with his lack of performance but he was a human being and was alive. I received a few quick pats but no big show was made. It was most important that the first mate be cared for and that the young officer not be humiliated. Here, in these spontaneous reactions by ordinary Cubans towards danger, non-performance and excelling was the essence of solidarity; just as the dictionary defines it: the union of fellowship. In the realization of this important human factor, one must appreciate what the Cuban revolution has done for the Cuban people, and therewith for the potential of the entire human race. Love takes precedence over work competency or bravery or "politics". Inadvertently, the Yankees, with their incessant aggression, have assisted the Cubans in solidarizing all the more with one another due to their collective need to be unified in face of that aggression.

In the remaining hours of the day, the first mate's broken wrist was set in a cast, the engine got repaired, in fact, and the crew settled back to normal. I was praised for my actions in the rescue, and no one ridiculed the remiss officer neither to his face nor behind his back. He kept to himself, but he came to the social salon when the purser announced that beer would be passed out.

Nothing untoward or exciting occurred during the few remaining days. But the evening before we arrived in Havana, there was a reunion. The captain, not prone to speak much, congratulated the entire crew for making the trip safely. He added that there had been more excitement than usual. He gave me a diploma for my voluntary work and I was named *destacado*. There were cheers and embraces, and two shots of rum each.

It is a permanent emotional loss when one loses his/her country. In my case, it was my choice to abandon the nation I was born in. Nevertheless, the loss of native roots bears heavily, if for no other reason than that one is estranged from one's close relations, and estranged from the lack of roots and close relations in the new land to which one immigrates. I never felt integrated or in any way Danish in Denmark. But in the time I was in Cuba I felt that this was my country, too, my revolution. There are many reasons to feel such, common ideology being one strong bond. But I could feel this connection, mainly, because the Cuban people I came to know allowed me to feel this, even helped me feel this. Their human warmth and idealism captured my heart. I felt it in many ways. One is the defense mechanism that takes over when confronted by condemnations of Cuba's revolution, whether it comes from foreigners—most often "journalists"—or from native Cubans. I find myself referring to Cuba as "our" land, of the revolution as "mine". Nor am I contradicted in this by Cubans who are supportive of the revolution. I am not talking about criticisms, they are often healthy, my own included of course. But, in the final analysis, it is the big question that counts: Which side are you on?!

One day not long after my last voyage, I met the first mate on a Havana street. He was standing beside a $ taxi with a chauffeur's cap on his head. His wrist was bandaged.

"Is that you...How's your wrist?" I asked, not wanting to believe what I was seeing.

"Yes. Good to see you, Ron. Well, my wrist is still healing but I can use it when driving."

"Why, why are you doing this? You had passed your captain's exams. You are still a young man. You would get your own ship."

"Yes, but I gave up sailing. I must feed my family. There is much more money in driving a taxi than in sailing."

These were the worst years of the special period. The hard economic times resulting from the fall of socialism in Europe brought with it a greater emphasis for many Cubans in finding individualistic economic solutions. The first mate had greater economic benefits than most Cuban workers but he, or his wife, wanted even more. I saw this tendency—the wanting more—as negative, as dangerous to the collective, to solidarity. But I could also see that the first mate was still a good man.

Within a couple weeks upon my return, I was working as a translator and writer for Latin America's first and largest international news bureau, Prensa Latina. Che Guevara had started this agency in the primitive setting of the Sierra Maestra mountains during the revolutionary war. Upon victory, Che started the process of organizing the little bureau into a major news agency. I was proud to be working in an organization Che had begun, and I was once again received in the spirit of solidarity.

Notes:

1. Friendly Cuban explicative. "Don't tell me. It's Ron."

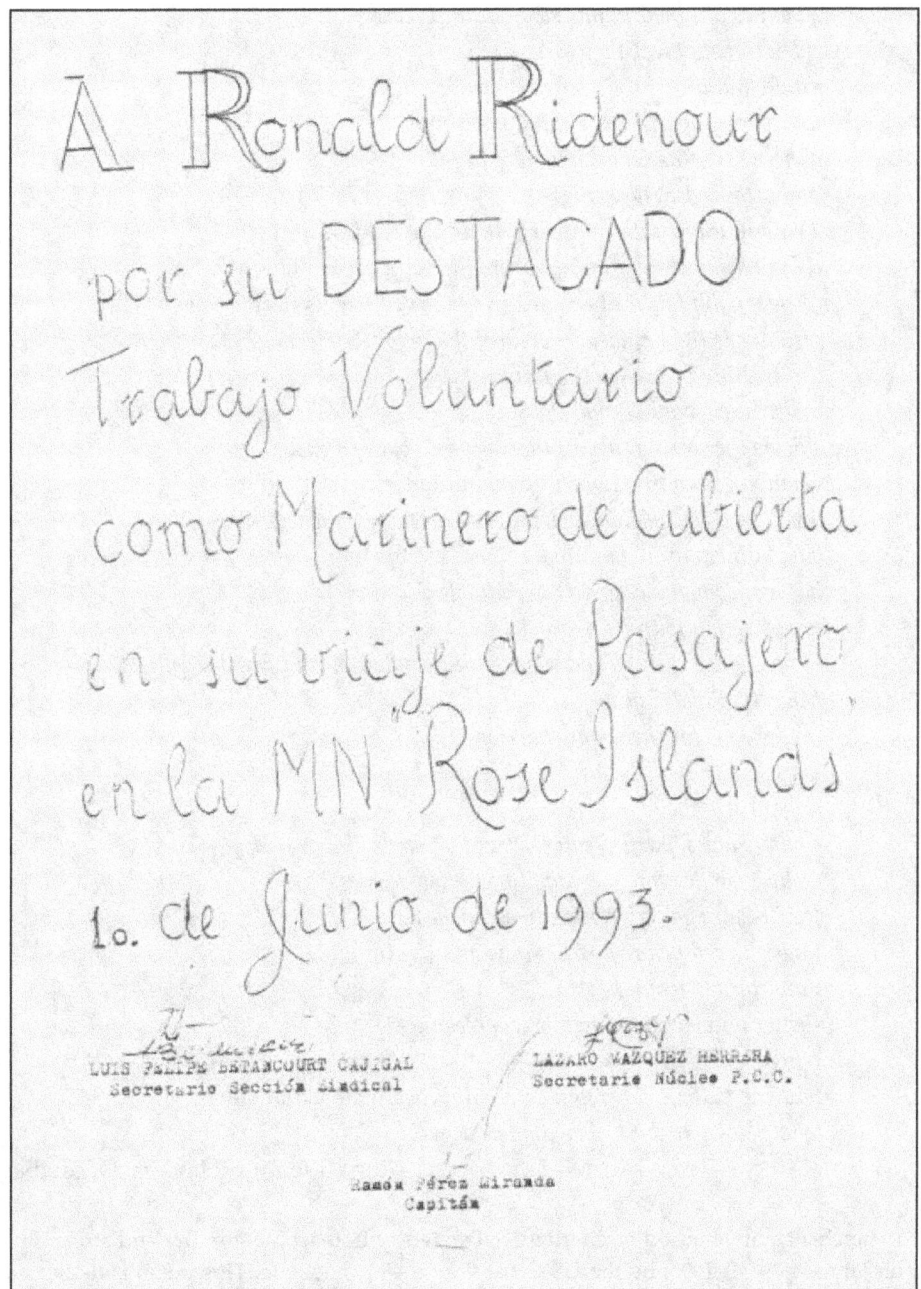

Figure 17: Diploma for the volunteer deckhand: 'To Ron Ridenour for his distinguished work as a voluntary deckhand on his voyage as a passenger on the ship Rose Island MN. 1 June 1993.'

CUBA: TENACIOUS ROYAL PALM

Avenues of Royal Palms sway in the breeze
splendrously erect they straighten
proud and tall
undulating trunk and pendulous fronds
dancing like the Guantanamera belle
immortalized in her song:
"Yo soy un hombre sincero de donde crece la palma".
("I am a sincere man from where the palm grows").
Royal palm faithfully rooted in fertile soil like its native sons
resolute as the implacable crew of the freighter Hermann (1)
unflinching before hostile thunder
whilst their noble Royal Palm
shields the sovereignty in the national coat of arms.
Changó god of fire, lightning and thunder
dines on chickens and pigs fattened on the palmiche berries (2)
cures illness with palm roots
has his women sweep dirt with its florescence
wraps cigars with its yagua bark (3)
builds house sidings and roofs with its palmitos and fronds (4).
Majestic Royal Palm
rendezvous for the ebony warrior
his svelte copper Ochún
elegant trio they:
Changó awesome fire-eater, ardent lover
Ochún goddess of rivers, deity of sensual love
Royal Palm gallery for godly escapades
umbrella rod before hostile rains and lightning
protector of farm lands
shelter for aborigini, mambi, campesino (5)
refuge for the tocororo
wearing Cuba's sovereign colors, this obstinate national bird
who chooses to die rather than be caged.

Ron Ridenour, Havana, December 1991

1. A Cuban merchant ship attacked in international waters with machine gun fire and streams of high-pressured water on January 30-31, 1990, by the US Coast Guard Chiconteague. This poem is dedicated to its crew who sailed onward to their Mexican harbor destiny with bullet holes in their hull and other damage.
2. *Palmiche* is the Spanish word for Royal Palm berries.
3. *Palmitos* is Spanish word for palm straw.
4. *Yagua* is the Cuban-Spanish word for Royal Palm bark.
5. *Mambi* was the resistance name for those Cubans who fought Spanish colonialism and later the US's neo-imperialism. *Campesino* is the Spanish word for small farmers.

www.ingramcontent.com/pod-product-compliance
Lightning Source LLC
Chambersburg PA
CBHW051213290426
44109CB00021B/2439